psycho kitty

PSYCHO KITTY

TIPS FOR SOLVING YOUR CAT'S "CRAZY" BEHAVIOR

Pam Johnson-Bennett, CABC

DISCLAIMER: This book is not meant to take the place of expert veterinary care. Because all behavior problems are case-specific and could have an underlying medical cause, consult your veterinarian for an accurate diagnosis. Any change in your cat's behavior could be an indication of a medical problem. Don't assume the problem is behavioral before consulting your veterinarian.

Celestial Arts
an imprint of Ten Speed Press
PO Box 7123
Berkeley, California 94707
www.tenspeed.com

Distributed in Australia by Simon and Schuster Australia, in Canada by Ten Speed Press Canada, in New Zealand by Southern Publishers Group, in South Africa by Real Books, and in the United Kingdom and Europe by Publishers Group UK.

Cover and text design by Betsy Stromberg
Front cover photo by ImageSource/Getty Images
Photo credits can be found on page 117

Library of Congress Cataloging-in-Publication Data

Johnson-Bennett, Pam, 1954-
Psycho kitty : tips for solving your cat's "crazy" behavior / Pam Johnson-Bennett.
p. cm.
ISBN 978-1-58761-323-4
1. Cats—Behavior. 2. Cats—Psychology. 3. Cats—Behavior therapy. I. Title.

SF446.5.J634 2008
636.8—dc22

2007039205

Printed in China
First printing, 2008

1 2 3 4 5 6 7 8 9 10 — 12 11 10 09 08

To Scott, Gracie, and Jack, with all of my love

TABLE OF CONTENTS

ACKNOWLEDGMENTS

I am continually impressed by the love and loyalty that my clients show to their cats. Through my work, I've had the pleasure of meeting some of the most caring people and the most incredible cats. Thank you all!

Thank you to my agent, Linda Roghaar, for years of friendship, wisdom, and support. I can never thank you enough for all you've done. I'm so proud to be able to call you my friend. Thanks to my publicist, Ellen Pryor. Thanks to the team at Yahoo, especially Robert, and to the outstanding team at Friskies for your belief in me. Thanks to Julie Kahn at Checkmark for making sure we all do our best. Thank you to my editor, Lisa Westmoreland, and my friends at Ten Speed Press. You made this a beautiful and fun project to work on.

INTRODUCTION

You've just adopted a dog—yes, a dog. You call a dog trainer to help the pup overcome some housebreaking problems, or maybe he needs training to stop his aggressive behavior toward strangers. None of your neighbors laugh at you or think you're crazy for calling in a trainer. In fact, they're thrilled at the thought of not having to live next door to an ill-mannered canine. On the flip side, tell your neighbors that you're calling someone to help you work on your cat's litter box or aggression problem and the giggling will reverberate throughout the neighborhood.

Ever since I decided to dedicate my life to helping people solve their cats' behavior problems, I've heard every excuse as to why it can't be done.

"Cats are untrainable!"

"Cats are too independent!"

"Cats do what they please!"

"Cats don't have owners, they have slaves!"

Many years ago when I was a brand-new cat owner, I too was under the impression that cats were untrainable, hairball-hacking creatures with their own agendas, and being well behaved was *not* on the list. But the more familiar I became with my cats, the more I realized that I *could* influence their personalities, strengthen the bond we shared, and correct behavior problems. The way a cat *thinks* began to fascinate me. It amazed me how little we know about the beautiful animals so many of us share our lives with. In general, cats were getting a bad rap!

I came upon this interesting career as an animal behavior consultant strictly by accident. In trying to solve the baffling behavior problems of my cats, I found myself delving deeper into animal behavior. I didn't want to merely correct what we label as "misbehavior"; I wanted to know *why* my cats did what they did. I started using behavior modification with my cats, then moved on to helping my friends solve their cats' problems. Before I realized it, I soon became a consultant to numerous veterinarians. Each year, more cats are euthanized for behavior problems than for any other reason. That's a very sobering fact.

In this book you'll view the world through the eyes of your cat. That's the secret to solving behavior problems. You can't truly correct a behavior problem until you discover the cause. By trying to see things as your cat does, you'll be able to let go of all those preconceived notions that he's misbehaving out of spite. That doesn't mean you have to crawl around on the floor, though I have instructed a number of my clients with new kittens to do just that in order to get a better perspective on kitten-proofing their homes.

In this book, I've used real cases to help illustrate diverse points of view: the frustrated owner, the kitty culprit, skeptical family members, and confused companion pets. I hope this approach will help you feel that you're not the only one going through a particular problem with a cat. It helps to know you're not alone.

Through these stories, you'll see the mistakes some owners make and how, with the correct behavior modification, we get the damaged cat-owner relationship back in sync. Sometimes it takes a while, depending upon how long the problem has been allowed to go on, but in most cases, the bond between owner and cat can be repaired and strengthened.

If your cat is displaying a behavior problem, then you're both probably living under tension. You look over at your kitty and picture the sweet, wonderful cat he used to be. Nowadays though, he's like a psycho kitty. You think to yourself, "Why is he doing this?" From the other side of the room, your kitty looks over at you with the same confusion, the same questions. Your living room may even start to resemble Dodge City at high noon—you on one side and your cat on the other. You stare at each other, waiting to see who will make the first move as everyone else in the house runs for cover.

The problem is communication between the two of you. Communication is always at the root of behavior or relationship issues, isn't it? If you've watched *Dr. Phil* or *Oprah* for even just fifteen minutes, you've learned that. When it comes to you and your cat, you're not speaking the same language. Most of us expect the cat to understand our ever-changing rules and seemingly endless verbal commands. And we certainly are a chatty species, aren't we? It's now time for you to learn his language. Trust me, it's easier than you think. Cats are very sensible and their rules are simple.

The stories assembled in this book will help you see the situation from the cat's point of view. Once you understand the cat's vantage point, you can apply that knowledge to solving behavior problems. Hopefully, though, you'll use the knowledge to head off problems before they even develop.

One term you'll see repeatedly throughout this book is play therapy. Basically, play therapy involves using an interactive toy (similar to a fishing pole, with string and a little toy dangling on the end). I like interactive toys, instead of the little furry mice toys that get thrown on the floor and forgotten, for several reasons. The interactive toy allows you to do just that: *interact* with your cat. It's a wonderful way to

strengthen the bond between you, build trust, help a timid cat blossom, or speed up the acceptance process between your cat and a new family member. Interactive play is also extremely valuable in dealing with aggressive cats because it can help the cat focus on an acceptable target. An added benefit is that the fishing pole keeps your hand at a safe distance from the cat's teeth and claws.

I use a positive approach to correcting behavior, and interactive toys are my secret weapon. Since cats are hunters, it's very hard for them to resist the sight of potential prey. A cat about to engage in an unacceptable behavior can usually be distracted with an interactive toy. Refocusing the impending unwanted behavior toward the toy makes a potentially negative situation positive. It may seem as if you're rewarding negative behavior, but you aren't, because you're refocusing the cat's behavior *before* the unwanted behavior actually occurs. Timing is everything in life, isn't it?

Interactive toys should be standard equipment for people who live with cats, as much so as litter boxes and food. One note of caution though: Be sure to put the toys away when playtime is over to ensure that your cat doesn't chew the strings. Putting the toys away also keeps them special for future play therapy sessions. You'll learn more about the different uses of play therapy throughout this book.

"My cat isn't normal!" I hear these words from people all the time. Perhaps you too suspect that your own cat isn't normal. Many people are convinced that their misbehaving cats can't possibly be normal; if they were, *why* would they be doing the unexplainable things they do? Oh, there surely are cats with abnormal problems, but most of the misbehaviors you'll experience with your cat are likely to be the normal kind. I know you don't believe me right now, but it's true.

Let's say your cat has rejected his litter box and is urinating and defecating on the carpet behind the sofa. Is that normal? If you said no, you'd be wrong. It is, in fact, a normal behavior. No, I'm not crazy; just stick with me on this. If the cat feels he can't use the litter box for whatever reason, he'll pick a spot that meets his needs. Now, just because I said that the behavior is *normal* doesn't mean that it's *acceptable*. But by realizing the behavior is a normal reaction for your cat, you can begin to solve the problem by finding the cause. Let's take the example of a litter box that's too dirty. Look at it in human terms: You're traveling by car and stop at a service station so you can use the restroom. When you go inside, you discover it to be filthy. You may grumble a few expletives, but you have the option of getting back in the car to try the service station across the street. Well, your cat doesn't have that option. If he goes to his litter box and finds it too filthy to use, he may feel the need, if desperate enough, to find a cleaner area. By recognizing that your cat is trying to solve a problem the only way he knows how, you'll abandon your old belief that he's deliberately misbehaving.

Another example of normal (but again, unacceptable) behavior in a cat is scratching the furniture. Scratching is a normal and essential part of cat life. Instead of punishing your cat, once you realize the behavior is normal and not deliberately destructive, you can set up a more acceptable scratching surface. Again, everybody wins!

Truly abnormal behaviors do exist, but these conditions require your cat to be under a veterinarian's care, perhaps in conjunction with a referral to a veterinary behaviorist. What we're going to cover in this book are those behaviors, big or small, that simply require some good old sleuthing by you. Just imagine how good it will feel to be able to impress your friends with the fact that you were able to figure out what's going on inside the mysterious feline mind of your cat.

CHAPTER ONE

MISSING THE MARK—litter box problems

For cat owners, I don't think there's a more misunderstood or more complex problem than when a cat stops using the litter box. Litter box problems run the full gamut, from slight to all-out war with that seemingly innocent plastic box. These three steps will help you sniff out the cause:

1. Get to know your veterinarian. Make sure the problem isn't medical (for example, lower urinary tract disease, renal failure, diabetes, hyperthyroidism, or geriatric conditions).

2. Think "inside the box." Check out the box itself. Is it clean? Let's be honest. If you were a cat, would you use that litter box? If not, it's time to roll up your sleeves and get out your scrub brush. Have you tried changing brands of litter? Is the box too small? Does it have a cover that might be restricting your cat too much? Is it in a high-traffic area? Is it located too far away? Is the number of boxes adequate?

3. Stress test . . . feline-style. Look for potential emotional causes: death, divorce, new baby, new pet, house renovation, change in your schedule—any crisis or change, however insignificant it may seem at the time.

THE DOMINO EFFECT

Gretchen, a one-year-old, thirteen-pound salt-and-pepper tabby, sat perched on the lap of one of her owners. Of the two, Eddie and Evelyn Clegg, Gretchen had wisely chosen Eddie—he had the larger of the two laps to rest on. Gretchen's large frame and abundant fur created quite a presence. She appeared nervous and apprehensive as I watched her eyes intensely remain fixed on Domino, the five-month old lab mix puppy who was busily chewing on a toy across the room. I had been called to the Clegg household because Gretchen had stopped using her litter box since the arrival of young Domino.

"We thought we were doing a good thing," explained Evelyn, as she sadly watched Domino happily chewing away on his toy, totally unaware of the chaos he had created since his arrival one month ago. Probably, from his point of view, life was an exciting adventure to be embraced with gusto. He wanted to be friends with everybody and hadn't yet gotten the hint that Gretchen didn't share his enthusiasm.

Learning to live with Gretchen had been a new experience for Eddie and Evelyn, both in their mid-sixties, as they'd never had a cat before. Their daughter, a cat lover who thought it was time they had a pet, had walked in one day with a present, a wiggling ball of fuzz.

Evelyn, who was seated on the couch next to me, leaned closer. "Eddie didn't care for the kitten at first."

Eddie interrupted. "That's not true," he defended himself.

"Edward William Clegg, that first night you said the kitten could stay in the kitchen but had to go back the next morning," she shot back at her husband.

"That's how *you* remember it." He sat up straight, and Gretchen released her stare on Domino just long enough to check on Eddie. He gave her a reassuring pat and she went back to puppy patrol.

Evelyn winked and continued with her story. "Gretchen wouldn't leave Eddie alone. She followed him everywhere. It was as if she knew she had to win him over." Her face softened considerably as she said, "They've been inseparable ever since."

So initially, all was wonderful in the Clegg home when little Gretchen became a member of the family. With their daughter's guidance, Eddie and Evelyn set up a litter box and scratching post. She instructed them on how to feed the new kitten, and she bought them a vast array of cat toys.

For months, life went along smoothly for everyone. According to Evelyn, Gretchen was blossoming into a beautiful cat with perfect manners.

Things changed with the sudden appearance of Domino.

"It all started because *he* gained too much weight," Evelyn said sternly as she pointed at her husband.

Eddie rolled his eyes, and I shifted in my seat. I didn't want to be brought into the middle of this age-old debate!

"You got fat. Admit it, will you?" Evelyn said, then continued, "The doctor said so." Her voice got just a bit louder for emphasis.

"And you've never gained weight?" Mocking her, he said, "Eddie, do I look fat in this dress? Eddie, do my hips look big? Eddie . . ."

Evelyn broke in. "Enough!"

The weight of one's spouse . . . scary subject. Even Gretchen decided to find other accommodations. She made a speedy exit off Eddie's lap and out of the room.

Evelyn turned her attention back to me. "Anyway," she went on, despite the obvious look of good-natured disapproval on her husband's face, "Eddie has put on forty pounds since we moved here, so his doctor put him on a strict diet. He also recommended that Eddie get some exercise every day—specifically, walking. Well, he did it for a week and then gave up. He said it was too boring. So, Laurie decided to get him a puppy. That way they could go on walks together."

According to Evelyn, Eddie looked forward to his walks with Domino. On the other hand, the arrival of Domino had been less copacetic for Gretchen.

I found Gretchen to be a sweet, playful cat. Domino was, well, a typical friendly, curious puppy looking for a good time. Unfortunately, when the two animals were together, Domino continually trespassed beyond what was obviously Gretchen's comfort zone. The more Domino tried to make friends, the more Gretchen rejected him. Evelyn and Eddie were understandably upset.

Evelyn gave me a tour of the house and showed me the spots that Gretchen chose repeatedly as her impromptu litter boxes. Both spots were in the dining room under the dining table. As we were approaching the bathroom, where Gretchen's litter box was wedged between the vanity and the tub, I noticed that Domino settled in the middle of the hall, halfway between the bathroom and the living room.

Just then, Gretchen came out of the bedroom and turned in the direction of the hallway. When she saw Domino, she stopped in her tracks. Domino's ears perked up and his tail began to wag. He was hoping for a game. Gretchen did an about-face and trotted into the living room. She settled on the highest perch, the headrest of the recliner. Domino's tail gave two hesitant wags before the puppy sank back down to the floor.

I explained to Evelyn and Eddie that although Domino looked relaxed and innocent as he lounged in the middle of the hallway, he was blocking Gretchen's safe passage to the litter box. He probably chose to camp out there because he knew this was a sure way not to miss the cat, should she go by. The problem was that Gretchen had become too intimidated to pass him. Therefore, her only option was to find a safer place for her eliminations. And it wasn't merely coincidence that her choice was in the dining room. This was the one room with three doorways: one to the kitchen, another to the living room, and a third to the hallway. By going under the dining table, Gretchen felt hidden, but the openness of the room provided her with a wide visual field. There'd be enough reaction time should she see Domino. The litter box in the bathroom was beside the vanity, hidden from the door, so Gretchen couldn't know if Domino was approaching until it was too late.

"In a multipet home, you have to be careful not to hide the litter box so far into a corner that it makes a cat feel helplessly trapped," I explained to the Cleggs as we stood in the dining room. "Look at the setup from your cat's point of view." I pointed to the different vantage points that the dining room offered.

"Does that mean we have to put the litter box under the dining room table?" asked a grim-faced Evelyn.

I shook my head, much to everyone's relief.

Behavior Plan

- ❏ **Blacklight sleuthing.** Check for any urine spots that may have been overlooked by using a blacklight. Its special bulb will cause urine stains to fluoresce. Blacklights are available at pet supply stores and online. Mark any spots with painter's tape, which is easy to remove, for later cleaning.

- ❏ **Destink.** Use a stain-removing and odor-neutralizing product on the areas. Use a product made especially for pet urine stains. Ordinary household cleaners will leave traces of urine odor that kitties can still smell!

- ❏ **Multiple choice.** Add a second litter box somewhere else in the house. In Gretchen's case, another litter box in the spare bedroom would provide her with more options.

- ❏ **Elbow room.** Place the box away from the wall and not wedged in a corner so the cat will feel she has escape options.

> Being in the litter box is not the time for a cat to have a surprise visitor. Be aware of potential ambushes when an unsuspecting cat is in the box.

- ❏ **No trespassing.** Restrict a new dog's access to the cat's litter box area. A hinged baby gate works well. As the dog becomes trained to stay out of the room, the gate can eventually come down, but in the meanwhile it will provide the cat some security.

> Create a cat-friendly gate by cutting a hole in a plastic mesh gate, just large enough for the cat to go through. For extra stability, glue or screw a wooden frame around the opening.

- ❏ **Creature comforts.** Create a safe, comfortable sanctuary where the cat can escape unwanted attention. Make it cozy by including a cat tree or window perch, a cozy bed, hiding places, toys, and so on.

- ❏ **Just like home.** Place a bit of soiled litter from the cat's original box into the new box to create familiarity.

- ❏ **Zen space.** Help the cat become comfortable with the new litter box setup. For the Cleggs, this means that after Gretchen eats, Eddie is to carry her

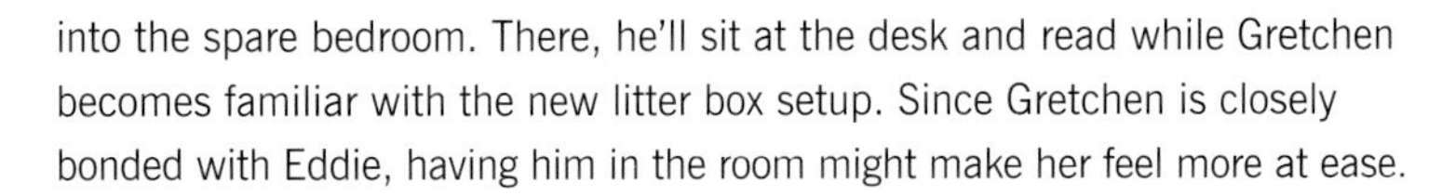
into the spare bedroom. There, he'll sit at the desk and read while Gretchen becomes familiar with the new litter box setup. Since Gretchen is closely bonded with Eddie, having him in the room might make her feel more at ease.

- ❑ **The high life.** Create elevated areas of refuge for the cat in the main parts of the house, such as cat trees or window perches. This will allow her to feel comfortable enough to stay in the room with her owners even if she doesn't want to be bothered by dogs (or small children!).
- ❑ **Pounce!** Engage in daily interactive play sessions using a fishing pole–type toy.
- ❑ **Control that pooch.** Engage in appropriate training of rambunctious canines, consulting a certified dog behavior consultant or qualified trainer if need be.
- ❑ **Give nature a hand.** Use Feliway Comfort Zone, a behavior modification product, in areas where the cat enjoys spending time.

> Feliway Comfort Zone is a behavior modification product that contains synthetic feline facial pheromones. These scent chemicals are identical to the ones your cat deposits when she rubs her face on objects. These pheromones, known as the "friendly pheromones," can help a cat feel more familiar and comfortable with her surroundings. Comfort Zone is available as a plug-in diffuser that covers about 650 square feet and lasts about a month. It also comes in a spray bottle used to stop urine marking. Both versions are widely available and come with complete instructions for proper usage.

Follow-Up

Providing an additional litter box for Gretchen made all the difference. She had no problem going through the gate and has used both litter boxes faithfully.

The cat trees became prime "no dogs allowed" real estate for this stressed-out kitty. Whenever she was unsure about Domino's intentions, she just hopped onto her cat tree and enjoyed the view. She'd sit at the top of the tree in the living room and observe him. Eventually, she'd sneak down to get a closer look, but knowing she could quickly be out of his reach made her feel secure, and this accelerated her acceptance of him.

The Cleggs engaged Gretchen in regular play therapy sessions, alternating a variety of toys. Not knowing which toy was going to make an appearance was the one unexpected surprise that Gretchen did enjoy. They also enlisted the services of a qualified trainer for Domino so he could learn some proper puppy etiquette. Gretchen and Domino have become close companions, but whenever they've had enough of each other and want some alone time, Gretchen heads for her cat tree penthouse and Domino stretches out on his monogrammed cedar bed. Just when he closes his eyes, Gretchen hops off the tree, saunters over, and curls up right beside him. Whether Domino is really asleep at that moment is anyone's guess, but the last time I was at the Cleggs' home, I thought I saw Domino give me a little wink as the cat nestled in close to him. Harmony in the Clegg house has been restored.

STINKY SECRETS

As cat owners sometimes do, Margaret Christensen became convinced that Stinky, her nine-month-old white kitten, was suddenly becoming spiteful. She first noticed a problem when Deborah, one of her three teenage daughters, mentioned that she saw Stinky urinating in the laundry basket. Filled with dirty clothes, the basket was sitting next to the washer. Deborah's discovery made Margaret recall that she routinely thought she smelled an odor similar to cat urine whenever she was in the laundry room. She had always dismissed it as being a bad combination of odors from the soiled laundry. After Deborah's discovery, Margaret whisked Stinky off to the veterinarian, who deemed the problem behavioral.

"I didn't realize the problem had gotten so bad," she told me over the phone, "until I was opening the windows in the sunroom the other day. I smelled something foul. I looked around and found piles of cat poop in the corner behind the potted plants."

After I arrived at the Christensen house, I was taken through the foyer toward the family room. As we passed the kitchen, I noticed a woman busily working away. A wonderful aroma of freshly baked chocolate chip cookies came from that direction. Margaret caught me enjoying the aroma. "Maria comes three days a week to do the cleaning, and she always bakes for us," she said.

At first my discussion with the Christensen family yielded nothing remarkable. No, there had been no changes to the house, everyone's schedules were basically consistent, and no traumas or stressful situations had come up recently. Basically, Stinky was a happy cat (or so they thought), living in a home with five very loving family members.

"Tell me about his litter box habits," I asked. "How often does he go, and do you notice anything particular about his behavior when he actually does use the box?"

I watched as the various family members looked from one to another. Deborah volunteered an answer: "I don't really ever see him in his box very much. He's pretty modest, I guess." The other family members nodded in agreement.

"Who routinely cleans the box?"

"We all scoop it out," Margaret replied, "I insisted that everyone be responsible for scooping each time they pass by."

As I continued my questioning, it seemed that no one could remember the last time they'd scooped anything out of the litter box. With so many people doing it, they each assumed someone else had already gotten to it and that's why the box was always clean. But somebody had to have scooped *something*, yet no one could remember doing so. This wasn't a good sign.

The best place to start solving this mystery was with the box itself. "This is Stinky's room. No one else uses it," Margaret proudly assured me as she turned on the light in the guest bathroom. What I saw was a major infraction of Rule #1 in cat etiquette. Stinky's litter box, though a good size and very clean, was only inches from his food and water bowls. For life and death reasons, a cat in the wild doesn't eliminate within his living area; that would be like putting out a huge welcome sign for predators. Even indoor cats who have never stepped so much as one pampered paw outdoors share that survival instinct. So Stinky faced a serious dilemma: he could either eat in the guest bathroom or he could use his litter box. Logically, since the food source was only in that one location, it narrowed down his choices. He had to seek out more appropriate bathroom facilities, away from his food.

Everyone was excited about making the necessary changes to help Stinky. One thing still bothered me, though. The number of times the family had discovered an inappropriately placed elimination and the number of times he should've eliminated (based on two meals a day) wasn't adding up. I grilled the family again as to who had actually cleaned what out of the litter box over the last several days, and still no one recalled anything specific.

"Stinky has to be going somewhere," I said, with different concerns running through my head. I feared that if we really searched every corner of the house, we'd find lots of hidden stains and messes. Margaret's jaw dropped when I voiced my suspicions.

"Well, let's look right away," she demanded as she looked worriedly from one family member to another. "Everyone take a different room."

We all spread out to complete this mission, not unlike a bizarre scavenger hunt. Stinky just watched from his perch on the back of the sofa. As I walked by, I quietly whispered, "Can I at least have a hint?" stroking his back in passing. But he wasn't giving up any secrets.

I passed the kitchen and absentmindedly glanced in at Maria, who was busily working away. She quickly looked up at me and then averted her eyes. Was it just my imagination, or did she try to avoid making eye contact with me? "Don't be silly, Pam," I thought to myself and proceeded on. Then it hit me. Back into the kitchen I went. Maria saw me and busied herself all the more.

"Maria," I began, "can I ask you a couple of questions about Stinky?"

Maria nodded, yet she continued with her work, which looked to be just arranging and rearranging objects on the counter. Why was she nervous?

"When you've been doing the cleaning, have you ever come across any of Stinky's messes?" I asked.

"No," she answered quickly.

"Are you sure?" I prodded.

Maria was silent for a moment, then looked toward the kitchen entrance before leaning closer to me. "I don't want to get Stinky in trouble," she whispered. "I love him and I'm afraid they'll get rid of him."

"So you *have* cleaned up after him?"

"Yes, many times," she answered, looking down. "He never uses his box. He always goes in the sunroom. I know all of his favorite spots so I clean them as soon as I get here."

I put my hand on her shoulder and told her not to worry. Maria's kitty cleanup confession gave me the information I needed to help him. I walked back to the Christensen family in the living room, ready to map out a strategy.

Behavior Plan

- ❏ **Operation stink finder.** Locate and clean all of the cat's favorite impromptu "litter box" areas.

- ❏ **The old switcheroo.** Relocate the food and water bowls away from the litter box area and monitor the cat as he becomes accustomed to the new dining location.

- ❏ **Follow the leader.** After dinner, guide the cat toward the litter box. (Stinky loves to follow Margaret anyway, so this will be easy for the Christensens.) Instead of placing him directly in the box, scratch around in the litter so the cat can hear it.

- ❏ **Take a detour.** If a member of the household even slightly suspects that the cat is considering relieving himself somewhere other than in his box, distract him with a toy and conduct a play session in the area where he used to inappropriately eliminate. This will help change his association with that area and also change his mind-set from negative to positive.

- ❏ **Sound effects.** Use clicker training to show the cat that good behavior gets rewarded.

- ❏ **Count to ten.** Don't use any form of punishment should someone come across an accident or actually catch the cat in the act. Punishment will only make the cat feel that the very act of elimination is bad. He won't understand that he's being punished for his choice of location. Every time he has the urge, he'll become nervous knowing that he might get into trouble. This will result in two things: First, a cat who resorts to finding more obscure locations. And second, a cat who's afraid of his owner.

A clicker is a small noisemaker that makes a cricket-type sound. You can buy clickers at your local pet supply store. You click whenever your cat does a positive behavior and then immediately offer a treat or food reward. The clicker marks the exact behavior so he knows what you want from him. The clicking sound becomes a cue to let him know that because he displayed the wanted behavior, he's going to get a treat immediately.

Start with pretraining to help the cat learn to associate the sound with the pending food reward: Place a piece of food in front of him, and when he goes for it, click the clicker. Do this several times a day for a couple of days, or until you feel your cat understands the connection between the clicker and the food reward.

Then you can begin the actual clicker training. Click and reward whenever he does something positive, such as walking by a previously urine-soiled area without an incident. Eventually, you can offer treats intermittently, so you won't always have to have food with you.

For step-by-step clicker training techniques, refer to my book *Starting from Scratch* (Penguin Books, New York, 2007).

Follow-Up

By appealing to Stinky's instinctual need to eliminate away from the nest, we were able to quickly retrain him. He began using his box again. He also responded so wonderfully to clicker training that the Christensens began teaching him some fun tricks. Stinky can now shake hands, roll over, and sit on cue. He has been renamed Stinky the Star by his family because of how much he loves to perform for visiting guests.

TOO LITTLE TOO LATE

Barbara Cunningham called me for an in-home consultation to address a litter box problem concerning her three young house-cats. All three cats had decided to stop using the box and elected to go on the floor beside it instead.

I went through all of the usual questions with Barbara on the phone. She'd already had all three cats checked by her veterinarian, she had more than one litter box, and she routinely cleaned them all. She hadn't had any change in her life recently. So we set up an appointment to try to solve the mystery.

When I entered the house, I was greeted by Barbara, a very attractive, well-dressed woman who looked to be in her mid-forties. Behind her stood her husband and two teenage sons. They were all looking forward to my uncovering the reason for their cats' supposedly strange behavior.

The three cats, all littermates, were nowhere to be seen. "They spend much of their time sleeping," offered Barbara as she noticed me looking around.

Barbara insisted on bringing me immediately to the litter boxes to view the "scene of the crime," as she put it. Now, there are times when cats stop using their litter box for emotional reasons, and it takes a lot of work on my part to figure out what went wrong. Then there are the cases like this one, where all it took was looking at the litter box conditions. The reason for the behavior was immediately apparent and the solution was simple. I hadn't even taken my coat off when I had the answer. This was a case of a picture being worth a thousand words—or meows in this case. I stood before two litter boxes, placed three feet apart in a combination laundry room/mudroom. The boxes were very tiny. Now with boxes that small, one would think Barbara's cats must be on the small side, but as it turned out, they were anything but petite.

Upon interviewing the family, I learned that all three cats got along beautifully. At nine months old, they all played, slept, and ate together.

When it came time to meet Ling Ling, Ming, and Yoki, I was confronted with three massive, waddling mountains of fur. When I entered the sunny bedroom where they spent most of their time, I was greeted with a mildly curious look from each before they decided I wasn't interesting enough for further investigation. All three cats laid their heads back down and continued to nap.

The problem came down to common sense—or lack of it. Here were the facts: three big cats with lots of *output* and two tiny litter boxes with too much *input*. Added to that, there was an insufficient amount of litter in each box. The solution required delicately reacquainting the Cunninghams with basic common sense. My theory behind the family's lack of attention to the litter box was "out of sight, out of mind." Litter box maintenance isn't anyone's favorite thing to do, so we look for all kinds of ways to reduce our exposure to it. Let's admit it—we *hate* to clean the litter box. That's why Barbara Cunningham put two small boxes in a part of the house that no one really uses. Barbara informed me that no one comes in through the mudroom door. She's the only one who goes back there, when she does laundry three times a week.

What the Cunninghams didn't take into consideration was the increased amount of waste that the cats would produce as they got bigger. Barbara didn't adjust the size of the boxes or the cleaning schedule as her cats grew . . . and grew . . . and grew. This brought up another point that we would still have to address—her cats were simply too fat. I asked Barbara about their diet and learned that she fed them home-cooked meals, based on the breeder's recommendation.

Behavior Plan

- ❏ **Deluxe accommodations.** Get larger litter boxes. Ideally, there should be a litter box on each floor of the house, but Barbara's husband won't agree to putting one on the second floor, so the Cunninghams' cats will have to make do with the one location.

- ❏ **Every inch counts.** Use enough litter to sufficiently cover the bottom of the litter box and allow for a few trips into the box to dig, eliminate, and cover. Barbara needs to pay attention to the fact that her three cats produce a large volume of urine and must spend a great deal of effort pushing the small amount of litter into the corner in an attempt to cover it. A general rule of thumb is to start with a three-inch layer and adjust accordingly based on the individual cat.

If your cat is very large and you can't find a litter box to suit her, purchase a plastic storage container. They come in many lengths and widths.

- ❏ **Scoop patrol.** Scoop the boxes several times a day. Set times for checking the litter boxes to help develop a routine. Nobody wants to use an unflushed toilet!

- ❏ **Moving mountains.** Schedule interactive play sessions on a daily basis. The Cunninghams' cats need a better quality of life. It's time for them to discover their inner kittens and enjoy playtime, rather than just naptime.

- ❏ **Room service.** Unless you really know what you're doing, home-cooked meals are seldom nutritionally appropriate for cats. Barbara should talk to her veterinarian about the cats' nutritional program and establish a healthy weight loss plan.

Cats must lose weight gradually to prevent serious liver damage. Work with your veterinarian to determine how much weight your cat needs to lose and how slowly it should be done. Sudden weight loss can result in hepatic lipidosis, a disease caused by fatty deposits in the liver.

Follow-Up

Barbara went out that evening to purchase new boxes and initiated a family scooping schedule. There have been no accidents since.

Ling Ling, Ming, and Yoki have gradually slimmed down on a veterinarian-prescribed diet that is nutritionally complete. Without all that extra weight, the cats have become more active and interact with the family more.

The lesson here is that sometimes we all need a reminder about common sense. I can think of lots of things I'd rather do than scoop the litter box, but it needs to be done and my cats count on me.

Remember to make adjustments as your cat grows and changes. Matching your cat's litter box to her size, age, and physical health is important. A tiny kitten may have trouble climbing over the side of a jumbo box, so start with a low-sided box and change it as she grows. A geriatric cat with arthritis may need a box with lower sides. The older cat may also need more boxes in convenient locations. And, remember to scoop, scoop, scoop. No unflushed toilets, please.

MAGIC CARPETS

A while back, I spoke at a public education seminar to benefit a local humane organization. When I walked in, I noticed that the room was quite crowded, and I was delighted that so many people were interested in learning more about feline behavior. I never know what to expect when I do these seminars because the topic of behavior modification for cats still causes much giggling and snickering. So when I saw that every seat was filled, I was very pleased.

I started by asking, through a show of hands, what problems people were having with their cats: litter box, aggression toward people, aggression toward companion pets, scratching furniture, stress or anxiety, jealousy, depression, finicky eating, and general training problems. Every hand went up when I mentioned the litter box. I scanned the room carefully to make sure I wasn't missing anyone, but indeed, everyone was raising a hand in the air. Some people held their hand up just a few inches, perhaps indicating embarrassment, while other people were waving their arms over their head and nodding, afraid I wouldn't notice them.

Realizing we had no time to waste, I put aside my notes on furniture scratching, aggression, and other behavior problems and began an in-depth discussion on litter box issues. As is usually the case, as I talked with the audience I discovered that many people were having problems because of some basic errors, such as only one box for several cats, unclean boxes, abrupt changes in litter types, food too close to the litter box, and so on. I had easy answers for those people.

In addition, there were two people at the seminar in search of answers to their litter box problems who had something in common: Their cats were reacting to the way something felt to their paws. That something was *carpet*. Here are their stories.

At thirty-six, Cole Anderson was finally at a point in his life where he had enough extra money to make some home improvements. Having grown up around cats, Cole decided the first improvement he needed to make in his home was to once again share it with a furry friend. His ex-wife had been allergic to cats, so during their six-year marriage he had accepted that the closest he'd get to having a cat would be to befriend the neighborhood tom who routinely raided his trash cans.

Now that his itchy-eyed ex-wife was gone and the tom had moved on to more interestingly filled trash cans, Cole was in search of a cat. As he read the morning paper, he took a quick look through the classified section to see if anyone was giving away a cat. Suddenly, there she was. Fate, destiny, whatever you want to call it, Cole knew he had found his cat even before seeing her.

> Free to a good home.
> Fifteen-month-old female cat.
> All shots up-to-date.
> Playful and affectionate.
> Must give away. Wife allergic.

It was the last two words that caught Cole's eye: *Wife allergic.* He grabbed the phone and dialed the number. The cat, a Manx named Winsome, was still available, and a short time later Cole brought her home.

Winsome took a little while to adjust to her new home. She remained slightly timid for the first two weeks, but with time, patience, and a box of cat treats, she warmed up to Cole.

Cole began his home improvement projects with Winsome's needs in mind. Included in his decorating plan was a tall cat tree that would sit in the front window. As Cole painted the interior of the house and added new furniture, he took great pains to ease Winsome through the process, and everything was going well as he entered the home stretch. The only thing left to do was install wall-to-wall carpeting in the bedroom. Cole decided to spoil himself and go for the expensive plush pile.

What Cole hadn't anticipated was that from the moment the carpet was installed, Winsome would begin using it instead of her litter box.

He took her to the veterinarian, who determined there was no medical cause for her behavior.

Cole put plastic sheeting down to cover the carpet, and during that time Winsome faithfully eliminated in the box. But as soon as the carpet was uncovered again, the problem resurfaced.

"Is she declawed?" I asked.

"Yeah," he answered. "I didn't have it done, though. Her previous owners did it."

"Are you using the same kind of litter that her previous owners used?"

"They were using some sandy kind of litter. I didn't want it tracked all over, so I'm using a pellet-type litter," he replied emphatically.

"Can you describe Winsome's routine when she's in the litter box?"

"Her *routine*?" He looked at me with a blank expression. "She pees and she poops. What else is there?"

I continued, "Does she spend a lot of time digging before she actually eliminates? Does she cover afterward or does she just hop in, take care of business, and bolt out of there?"

I could see by Cole's expression that I had struck a chord. "She jumps in and perches on the very edge, then jumps right out. She never actually covers with the litter."

Aha! Winsome, a declawed cat, was used to the soft feel of the scoopable sand litter. When she went to live with Cole and had to use the rough, hard pelletized litter, she tried to limit her contact with it. Some common signs that a cat may be uncomfortable with the litter substrate include perching on the edge of the box, not covering, and zooming out of there. The cat may also attempt to cover by scratching at the walls or floor around the box. Now, not every cat who doesn't cover is unhappy with the litter, but in Winsome's case the pieces of the puzzle all seemed to fit together: The soft plush carpet in the bedroom probably reminded Winsome of the way the sand litter felt. The carpet met all of Winsome's requirements. It was soft, absorbent, and it didn't bother her sensitive paws.

Behavior Plan

- ❏ **Day at the beach.** Try a different kind of litter; in Winsome's case, that would be the scoopable litter she's used to. To address Cole's concern with tracking, he should switch to one of the low-tracking formulas. He should also keep the carpet covered for a while so Winsome has time to make the connection with the way her paws feel in the new litter.

- ❏ **The nose knows.** Thoroughly clean all soiled areas using an odor neutralizer.

Texture is very important to a cat. An unfamiliar litter with a texture different from what the cat is used to can cause substrate aversion.

- ❏ **Plug in some comfort.** Use Feliway Comfort Zone in areas inappropriately used for elimination. The feline facial pheromones in Comfort Zone will help the cat identify the space as a living area, not a litter box area.

The other interesting carpet-related problem had to do with a woman who was completely at her wit's end with the seven-year-old stray she'd adopted two months earlier. Peggy Bosh had tried everything, she said, to train her cat to use a litter box. "He just won't use it," she said with a sigh. "My veterinarian said there's nothing wrong with him. He just doesn't know what the box is for."

"What training methods have you tried?" I asked.

"Everything!" she answered.

I smiled. "Can you be a bit more specific?"

Peggy related how she had found this smelly, filthy, gray stray cat inside her car. Just before she went to bed one night, she remembered that she'd forgotten to close the car window and it looked like rain. She put her slippers on, threw a robe over herself, and darted out to the driveway. As she opened the door, she saw a pair of eyes staring at her from the front seat. It was hard to say who was more startled, Peggy or the skinny little gray cat who bolted out the open door.

Padding back toward the house in her fuzzy slippers, she was surprised to find the cat sitting on the back porch watching her. She thought for sure he'd run as she got closer, but he held his position. Peggy walked by him and into the house, certain he'd be gone in a few minutes.

Just before she got into bed, she took a quick glance outside to see if the cat had gone. There he was, still sitting on the back porch, looking in at her. Peggy turned out the light and went to bed.

It was after the third large boom of thunder that Peggy got out of bed and went back to the kitchen to look out the back door. When she flicked on the light, she saw that the driving rain made her driveway look more like a river. When she looked onto the back porch, she saw the same gray cat staring at her, only this time he was soaking wet.

Despite her better judgment and fears about having fleas in her carpet, Peggy brought the cat inside.

In her robe and slippers, she searched the basement for the bag of cat litter that she kept for winter emergencies, in case her car got stuck in ice. Having found that, she rummaged some more until she found an old dishpan to use as a litter box. Filling the pan with litter, she placed it in the kitchen. She also put down a bowl of water and searched through the refrigerator for some leftover chicken for her guest.

The last thing Peggy did before going back to bed was to put an old blanket down on the floor for the cat. Then she closed the door that separated the kitchen from the rest of the house, and off to bed she went, not certain but fairly sure she had just adopted a cat.

After a trip to the veterinarian that included a much-needed bath, the gray cat Peggy had adopted turned out to be white.

"The night I found the cat, I knew that if I kept him it would be a struggle to teach him house manners and it was," Peggy said. "I've managed to get him to stop stealing my dinner and he's becoming very affectionate, but he just doesn't get the idea of the litter box. He simply targets one spot in the home—the carpet in my home office and den."

Oscar didn't have accidents in any other part of the house, and he wasn't the least bit interested in any of the other rugs or the floor. He'd decided that the plush carpet in Peggy's home office and den was perfect for his needs. He refused to compromise.

All eyes in the auditorium were upon me, wondering if I could solve this three-month problem in just three minutes. I pronounced, "Oscar, it seems, has made his own determination, and you can either battle with him or you can let him have his way. I vote for the latter."

Everyone stared at me. Had I lost my mind? Was I suggesting that Peggy allow Oscar to ruin her carpet?

"What are you saying?" she asked with wide eyes.

"Do you have any carpet scraps left over?" I asked.

"Yeah, in the basement," she replied.

"Let's try an experiment," I said, and began to lay out the plan.

Behavior Plan

- ❑ **Ooh, that feels nice.** Cut a piece of the carpet scrap and put it in the litter box—just the carpet, no litter. Each day, sprinkle a little litter over the carpet scrap. Replace the scrap as it gets soiled. Don't add too much litter; just sprinkle a small amount as the cat makes the adjustment.
- ❑ **Ooh, this doesn't feel so nice.** Keep the carpet the cat was soiling covered with plastic for a week or so.
- ❑ **The incredible shrinking carpet.** As the cat begins to use the box, gradually make the pieces of scrap carpet smaller and smaller. Eventually there will be more litter and less carpet, making it a gradual and painless transition for the cat.

A commercial litter called Cat Attract is formulated with special herbs to entice cats to use the box. It can be very helpful in issues relating to the litter box. The product is widely available at pet retail stores.

Note: I qualified my recommendations to both Cole and Peggy by adding that this was my three-minute seminar answer to their problems, and without actually doing a house call it was impossible to be certain of the cause of the behavior. Both owners understood that, but at least they felt they now had a possible solution that made sense.

If you think your cat may have an aversion to her current type or brand of litter, set out an additional box with another type. You can even set out a third type in yet another box to see which she prefers—a litter box buffet, so to speak.

Follow-Up

With seminars, I don't always get the opportunity to follow up on how my recommendations work out, so I was thrilled when I later heard from both Peggy Bosh and Cole Anderson.

In a letter, Peggy wrote that the carpet scrap method worked like a charm. She admitted that she felt foolish doing it at first, and that Oscar initially looked at her suspiciously, as if he thought it must be a setup. But after a week, Oscar was using his litter box as if he'd been doing so all his life.

Cole Anderson phoned me four days after the seminar to say that it must have been the sand litter that Winsome needed, because she used it immediately and went through the ritual of covering afterward.

"Does she still perch on the edge of the box?" I asked.

"No," he answered. "She goes right in the middle now."

Comfort matters!

CHAPTER TWO

TOOTH AND NAIL—aggression

A question I'm asked all too often is "Why does my cat bite?"

Aggression is such a complex problem. When answering this question, I always recommend that the person first consult the cat's veterinarian, and then, if no medical cause is determined, contact a certified behavior expert. A truly aggressive cat is dangerous. The realization that your little purring ball of fluff can mysteriously transform into a cat from a Stephen King novel is terrifying. But people often label their cats aggressive and mean when, in fact, they aren't.

Aggression requires you to put aside your subjectivity and look at the situation through your cat's eyes. Is your cat truly aggressive across the board, or is she acting aggressively under certain conditions? There are many types of aggression; can you isolate which one your cat displays? Is she showing fear aggression, say, at the veterinarian's office? Or is she showing play aggression when she gets too carried away during playtime? Does she get aggressive toward you whenever she sees another cat outside the window? If so, she may be exhibiting redirected aggression. There are several other types of aggressive behavior, but I think you get my point. Determining the conditions surrounding the behavior is crucial to solving the problem.

Some cases of cat aggression are very sensitive because both the cat and the family are in crisis. There are times when the family has become so frightened of the cat that even if I'm able to solve the aggressive behavior, I then have to work with the family to reestablish their trust of the pet. More often though, aggression is caused by miscommunication, meaning the owner doesn't understand what the cat is feeling, and thus misreads warning signs.

TOO HOT ESPRESSO

Miscommunication was a big part of the problem that Barry Turner and his cat Espresso were experiencing. Barry called me to help with what he described as his cat's very aggressive behavior. It seemed that Espresso, Barry's much-loved cat, had become consistently aggressive toward anyone who entered the house. When Espresso was alone with Barry, he was loving and gentle, but toward any and all guests, he became a growling, stalking, hissing alien creature who would unexpectedly sink his sizable canine teeth into the closest hunk of human flesh.

Do I sound a bit dramatic? Well, realize that Espresso so terrorized Barry's friends that they would no longer come over until they'd been assured that "Evil Espresso" was safely locked in the bedroom. Barry's social life steadily plummeted. Having a girlfriend over to the house was

out of the question. Even Barry's parents and younger sister refused to visit unless Espresso was incarcerated. Despite the ridicule and criticism everyone heaped on Barry, he refused to give Espresso up, even though he certainly wasn't pleased with the cat's behavior.

When Barry phoned me, he'd already taken Espresso to the vet, who told him the aggression had no medical cause. I sent a behavior history questionnaire to Barry just after our phone conversation. The answers on the questionnaire provided valuable clues as to why Espresso's behavior had changed.

Barry had moved twice since getting Espresso. The first time was just three months after he brought the cat home. Because he was waiting for his new house to be completed and the lease had expired on his apartment, he temporarily moved in with a friend. There, Barry and Espresso had the run of the house but shared the space with Barry's friend and his wife and two children (boys, aged seven and nine), as well as two very opinionated, nonstop Yorkshire terriers. In the behavior questionnaire, Barry admitted that Espresso spent most of those four months under the bed or in the closet. Because the construction of the new house took up most of Barry's free time and attention, Espresso was pretty much on his own.

Regarding Espresso's aggression, Barry wrote that it shocked him because all of his friends had been crazy about the cat at first, when he lived in the apartment. Each person greeted Espresso upon arriving at Barry's home, and he was always the recipient of much petting. He was such a friendly kitten that many of Barry's friends loved to hold him and sought him out whenever they visited. Of course, that quickly changed when Espresso's personality took such an ugly turn.

When I called Barry to arrange a time for our consultation, he assured me that Espresso would be locked up prior to my visit.

"I don't want him locked up," I replied.

"What?" Barry responded with shock.

"Just let him go normally about his day. Don't worry about how he'll react to me."

"Are you sure you want him loose? What if he attacks?" he asked.

"I've been doing this a long time. I can handle myself with Espresso, believe me. Anyway, I don't think he'll go after me," I assured him, but I knew my words provided zero comfort.

Based on the history Barry provided, how I behaved upon entering the house and the way Espresso reacted to me would serve as the first behavior modification lesson—for both Barry and Espresso.

I rang the bell and the door was barely cracked open.

"Hello, it's Pam," I whispered into the inch of darkness.

"He's loose," came a nervous voice from the other side of the door.

"That's okay," I assured him.

With that, Barry let down his guard and opened the door. I stepped inside, and he instantly shut the door behind me.

"Let's sit down," I suggested. Nodding in reluctant agreement, Barry led me into the living room. Before sitting down, he took one last look around for Espresso.

The cat finally appeared just as we sat down. Espresso glared at me from across the room but made no move other than blinking his expressive eyes. He remained that way for several minutes.

We three held our positions for a good ten minutes. I made no direct eye contact with Espresso, I kept my body posture relaxed, and I didn't engage in any major movements as I sat. I was careful to not use expressive hand gestures as I talked. I kept my voice calm and quiet. Then, as Barry watched in disbelief, Espresso sauntered over toward me and began sniffing my shoes. He then moved on to inspect my purse. Suddenly, the fishing pole toy lying nearby on the carpet caught his eye. He tentatively pawed at it while periodically keeping an eye on me. I made no move to pick up the toy to play with him. I wanted him to take as long as he needed to evaluate the situation.

"He's never this calm," Barry said quietly without taking his eyes off Espresso. Temporarily satisfied with his investigation, Espresso retreated out of sight.

For a cat who normally would have been aggressive toward a visitor, his behavior was just what I'd been hoping for. And how I helped him achieve it was no magic trick—I simply let him take control. This seemed to be something he'd been unable to do of late.

The move Barry had made to his friend's house was a rough transition for Espresso. He lost his familiar territory, and to top it off, his new surroundings posed many threats, including the boys. Espresso had never been exposed to children before. From Barry's description of life at his friend's house, the kids were used to playing frantic chase games with their two dogs. When Espresso came on the scene, the boys chased him too, thinking he'd enjoy it as much as the dogs did (though I wonder just how much the Yorkies actually enjoyed the game). When the boys weren't chasing Espresso or hunting him down, the dogs were. Espresso became reclusive, preferring to hide in the closet of Barry's bedroom with eyes as big as saucers.

The next move, to yet another unfamiliar place, sent him into hiding for a week. The unpacking of boxes and the related chaos kept Espresso huddled in the back of the closet, exiting only long enough to eat and use his litter box.

Barry's best friend, Danny, came for a visit a few days after the move. When the doorbell rang, Barry threw open the door and the two friends greeted each other in their usual boisterous way. But the levity ended when Danny bent down to scoop up his old pal Espresso, only to be greeted by what sounded like a war cry and a frenzy of teeth and claws. The encounter landed Danny in the emergency room.

The next day, Espresso seemed to be his old self again. Whatever caused his cat to act that way was hopefully in the past, Barry thought. Yeah, right!

A trip to the veterinarian revealed Espresso to be in fine health. A prescription for Valium was dispensed, and home Barry and his cat went, hoping to get on with life again. Valium did little to control Espresso's aggression toward visitors. He managed to corner Barry's new girlfriend in the bathroom. When her screams brought Barry racing to her aid, he found her standing on the toilet, batting at a hissing Espresso with a towel.

After a few more similar episodes, Barry was convinced that if he didn't keep Espresso incarcerated he would have no friends left. Was Espresso doomed to being locked up eternally? Would Barry ever be able to have a normal social life? Was Espresso truly an attack cat? Barry looked at me as if I held the answers to his whole future.

Espresso's aggressive behavior was probably due to having been under constant attack in their interim home. In Barry's friend's house, Espresso hardly had a corner to himself. He was constantly barraged by dogs, children, strangers, and totally unfamiliar surroundings.

> I've always held the theory that many cats gravitate toward guests who are either allergic or not interested in them. That type of visitor will just sit on the sofa and ignore the kitty. This gives the cat time to get a closer look without worrying about being grabbed, so he'll feel more in control and less threatened.

When they moved to Barry's new house, Espresso had to adjust to yet another totally unfamiliar situation. Maybe in his mind, the best defense was a good offense. Unsuspecting visitors would go right up to Espresso, unaware that he needed adjustment time to evaluate and investigate who was entering his territory. Scent is very important to cats, so imagine how crucial it is for them to be able to inch closer at their own pace in order to investigate. That's why I was pretty sure that Espresso wouldn't attack me when I went on the consultation. I led him take the lead, and I made sure my body language reflected that I posed no threat.

Behavior Plan

- ❑ **A new outlook.** Help the cat regain his territorial security. Conduct daily play therapy sessions in all areas of the house to help the cat associate positive things with every inch of his territory. For Espresso, the bulk of the sessions should be conducted in the living room and the foyer just inside the front door, since these areas represent the greatest threat and hold the most negative associations.

- ❑ **Just a click away.** Use clicker training (described in chapter 1) to give the cat a mission and help him focus on good behavior.

- ❑ **Make nice.** Bring someone into the house in a nonthreatening way. This person should sit quietly on the sofa, avoiding direct eye contact with Espresso, allowing the cat to take control. Keep an interactive toy handy in case diversion is needed keep the cat focused on the positive. The principle of the exercise is to let the cat gradually feel less threatened. In Espresso's case, since he responds positively to me, I will be the "visitor" the first few times. If all goes well, the next step is to include one of Barry's friends, with me still there to act as a bridge between the familiar and the frightening.

> In addition to providing elevated areas, it can also be helpful to create hiding places so your cat can check out the goings-on in a room and not feel so exposed. For some cats, though, that hiding place may need to be in another room altogether. If your cat feels too threatened by guests, make life easier on everybody by placing him in another room when company comes to visit.

- ❑ **Find your happy place.** Turning to environmental issues (the cat's, not the world's), make the living room a less threatening, more cat-friendly place. Purchase a multitiered cat tree and place it near a window to serve as the cat's own personal piece of furniture. The cat tree, as opposed to the sofa and chairs, will have the cat's own comforting scent. This way, if he feels apprehensive about a visitor but still curious, he can safely stay in the room on his own tree—a territory within a territory.

- ❑ **Something in the air.** Use a Feliway Comfort Zone diffuser (described in chapter 1) to help the cat feel a little more at ease in the environment.

Follow-Up

Espresso responded to play therapy with the enthusiasm of a kitten. At first he was nervous, presumably looking for signs of danger (the Yorkies or the children). But as soon as he realized that the "prey" was his and his alone, a whole new world opened up to him—life was actually fun! He also took to clicker training, which helped him stay focused. He became a cat eager to please instead of a cat eager to attack. Barry purchased two cat trees, one for the living room and one for the bedroom, and Espresso wasted no time in claiming them.

My training visits were well received by Espresso. Eventually, I was able to initiate play using his favorite interactive toy. After the game Espresso stayed close to me, stretching out on the far end of the sofa—quite a big step for him.

Ten months after my last visit, Barry called with a glowing report. To avoid any potential threats and to allow his cat adequate investigation time, Barry continues to request that guests not approach Espresso or make direct eye contact.

By the way, Barry wanted to make sure I let you know that his social life is great now. Espresso likes his girlfriend and the future is looking good.

In the animal world, a direct stare can be interpreted as a challenge. When meeting a cat who appears to feel threatened, never look directly into his eyes. Offer him the comfort of knowing you pose no threat.

THE RACCOON INCIDENT

If your cat has ever displayed redirected aggression, you know how scary it can be. This behavior occurs when a cat is upset by something and can't get to the primary source of his agitation. As a result, he lashes out (literally) at the person, cat, or dog nearest him. Unsuspecting cat owners and companion animals have often been the targets of an agitated cat's redirected aggression.

The most common example of redirected aggression among companion cats occurs when a strange cat makes a sudden appearance in the yard. For instance, two companion cats who have peacefully lived in the same house for years may be sitting by a window watching the birds. Suddenly, an unfamiliar cat appears in the front yard. The two cats looking out the window become very nervous. One of the cats begins to growl, and then in a flash he lashes out at his buddy, teeth and claws bared. If you're lucky, the confused cats recover from this crisis relatively quickly. If you're not so lucky, or if the original source of the problem continues to cause agitation, the relationship between the companion cats deteriorates.

If the cats are separated immediately after the incident, there's a good chance that all will be forgotten by the next morning. Unfortunately, in many of the cases I'm called about, the cats were left together and, as a result, remained agitated with one another. Long after the true source of the trouble has left the yard, the two hapless companions remain at odds with each other.

Such was the case with Pebbles and Bam-Bam, two domestic shorthair cats. The two littermates had been rescued at the age of five weeks by Roger Beresford. Mr. Beresford, a confirmed bachelor at the age of sixty-two, had been sharing his quiet life with Pebbles and Bam-Bam (given those names by his niece) for the past ten years. The two cats

were inseparable, often sleeping so tangled up together that Mr. Beresford found it impossible to tell where one cat left off and the other began.

Peace and harmony came to a screeching halt one evening when an uninvited raccoon began working a small hole in the screen on the kitchen door. Bam-Bam was having a little snack at the food dish when he turned and came face-to-face with the furry bandit. Bam-Bam's loud meow sent the raccoon scrambling away and brought Mr. Beresford running from the living room to see what was going on. Pebbles tiptoed in behind him, curiously peering from behind his leg.

Bam-Bam, with tail puffed, inched toward the kitchen door, growling and hissing. Not having ever seen her brother act that way before, Pebbles delicately walked over to him and was instantly pounced upon in a frenzied attack. Within seconds, Pebbles flew from the room with Bam-Bam in hot pursuit, a hunk of her fur trapped in the corner of his mouth.

Two months after that incident, I was called because things had gone from bad to worse. Mr. Beresford said he had tried everything. Whenever he caught Bam-Bam stalking Pebbles, he would squirt him with water or clap his hands. Now things had progressed to the point where they could barely be in the same room together.

"If things don't improve, I'll have to give one of the cats away," Mr. Beresford said, his eyes fixed on Bam-Bam, who lay grooming himself on an overstuffed chair nearby.

"Pebbles was, unfortunately, in the wrong place at the wrong time," I began, "and because Bam-Bam was so agitated, he redirected his aggression to the closest target. When cats aren't separated shortly after a traumatic episode like the one you've described, the tension can remain quite high between them. As a result, each cat is no longer acting the way the other is used to, making them defensive toward each other. As time goes by, the original cause of the problem, the raccoon, isn't even a factor. From each cat's point of view, the other cat is now a threat."

In my tour of the house, I found one litter box that both cats had shared in the past without a problem. Even though Mr. Beresford reported that there had been no spraying or urinating outside the box, he did inform me that Bam-Bam would wait outside the bathroom door whenever he heard Pebbles scratching around in the litter. When she jumped out of the box, he'd pounce on her, causing her to run back to the master bedroom, her sanctuary. I told Mr. Beresford that he was lucky, because from what he described, a litter box problem was very close to surfacing. Being under a constant threat and having only one option when it came to the litter box could soon drive Pebbles to seek safer, more secluded areas.

I explained in detail how redirected aggression works and how the intense feelings from that one traumatic episode had snowballed into constant day-to-day tension. What we needed now was a solid behavior modification plan, patience, and no more attempted break-ins from Rocky Raccoon.

Behavior Plan

- ❑ **Take five.** Give each cat some breathing room. In this case, Pebbles shouldn't live in fear every time she has to use the litter box, and Bam-Bam shouldn't feel that his very existence is threatened by having another cat in the same house. A few days' relief is needed. Set up a separate living space for each cat with a litter box in each area.

- ❑ **Coach each player.** During the separation, work on increasing each cat's self-confidence. Yes, I know that sounds silly, but it helps. Use interactive play therapy and positive association. Convey it in a language that they'll understand by triggering the prey drive. Use what nature has already provided . . . well, sort of. We're not talking real prey here, so relax. Look at a cat as what he is—a predator. If he's successful in his captures, he becomes a more confident cat. For Bam-Bam, these play sessions would help redirect some of his aggressive energy into something positive. They would also allow him to feel confident by making him feel like a successful hunter—without resorting to bullying Pebbles.

- ❑ **Hide-and-seek.** Since cats like to hide behind trees, bushes, and rocks as they inch closer to their prey, provide adequate cover during playtime by setting out boxes, open paper bags, or anything else the cat can use for cover while silently sneaking up on the "prey." For a nervous or timid cat, such as Pebbles, being able to hide behind a box in the middle of the room will also help her venture out into the center of the room. She'll be so distracted in her pursuit of the toy that she won't realize she has expanded her comfort zone.

- ❑ **Smooth moves.** Interactive play therapy should not be merely a physical game. The cat should engage both mentally and physically. We don't want this to be an exhausting and frustrating chase, but rather a stimulating, exciting, and rewarding hunt. Move the toy like prey so the cat will respond as a predator. That means moving the toy away from the cat (a mouse certainly wouldn't run toward the cat) and alternating movements with staying still.

- ❑ **Victory!** In order to boost confidence, cats need to have captures, so make sure the cat successfully captures the prey several times during each game. Toward the end of the game, slow down the movements of the toy to simulate exhausted prey, and at the end of the game allow one final grand capture. That will help leave the hunter more satisfied and relaxed at the end of the play session. Don't you wish that it was that easy and fun to boost our own confidence?

- ❑ **Peek-a-boo!** Once the cats are comfortable and back to normal while still separated, begin having them view each other at a distance. Do this for only a few seconds at a time, using food or treats for distraction. They need to associate each other with the appearance of something positive. I don't know about you, but the appearance of food is always positive to me.

- ❑ **Stay dry.** To help the cats form positive associations with each other, don't punish them when they have a negative encounter. Mr. Beresford should stop squirting Bam-Bam with water when he stalks Pebbles. That will only add to their apprehension about one another and continue the cycle of anxiety. Use the positive association technique instead.

- ❑ **Watch the clock.** Gradually increase the length of time that the cats view each other as the sessions progress successfully.

- ❑ **Ambience.** Use Feliway Comfort Zone (described in chapter 1) to help alleviate stress and anxiety. Also, create more options for escape and sanctuary in the home. Set up cozy hiding places for private naps, elevated areas for scoping out the room, and more than one option for attending to business in the litter box. An additional litter box may ease tension if either cat feels the potential for ambush.

To prevent overcrowding, it's a good idea to have the same number of litter boxes as you have cats. This can also help if one cat feels territorial toward a particular box. The litter boxes should be set up in various parts of the home, not all lined up in one location.

Follow-Up

Mr. Beresford soon became adept at conducting play therapy sessions that were nothing short of feline fantasies. The increased enrichment of their environment and their gradual reintroduction to one another helped them put the past behind them.

Because Bam-Bam showed that he has the potential for redirected aggression, Mr. Beresford has also become more aware of whether a tense situation might be brewing. If Bam-Bam is looking out the window at something and appears agitated, Mr. Beresford casually but quickly whisks Pebbles into another room and distracts Bam-Bam until the coast is clear.

HE SAID SHE SAID

I received an urgent call on my cell phone from an animal hospital in town.

"Dr. Fields is in the exam room," the veterinary technician said in a rush of words as soon as I answered. "He asked me to call you because a married couple is here with a cat for vaccinations. The wife is yelling at the husband. She wants the cat put down. The husband refuses to do it. Is there any chance that you can get here?"

When I arrived at the clinic, I was ushered into the back lab area, where I saw Dr. Fields.

"Hi, Pam. I'm sorry to do this to you," he said.

"What do you want *me* to do?" I asked, glancing toward the door to the eerily quiet exam room.

"According to Mrs. Stanley, their cat, Ebony, has been showing more aggression at home. She doesn't want the cat anymore. The husband loves Ebony and refuses to do anything. He thinks Ebony is aggressive because Mrs. Stanley hates him. They came here for vaccinations, but I think Mrs. Stanley agreed to come because she wanted to convince me to euthanize Ebony. This cat is always very aggressive in our clinic, but this time he surprised everyone and lashed out at Mrs. Stanley instead of me. She has a couple of big scratches on her arm, and that's only adding more conviction to her argument for getting rid of the cat."

"Do they want a consultation?" I asked, not looking forward to working with a couple on opposite ends of the cat tolerance scale.

"They don't even know that I called you. There's nothing wrong with the cat, other than the fact that he hates coming here and they have a difficult time wrangling him into the carrier. I have no idea why he's become aggressive at home. His physical exam checks out normal. You can take as long as you need," he offered. "The exam room is yours."

"Thanks," I said, with the type of smile one might offer if invited to enter a snake pit.

Once in the exam room, I smiled at Mr. and Mrs. Stanley, staked out in opposite corners of the room. Mrs. Stanley was holding some gauze to her arm. I was greeted in return with a hopeful smile from Mr. Stanley. Mrs. Stanley, on the other hand, was . . . well, let's just say that her side of the room was a bit frosty.

The blue plastic carrier sat on the floor between them. From where I stood, the only thing I could see was a dark shadow inside. Although the room appeared calm—tense, but calm—there were telltale signs of the recent trauma. Dark puffs of cat hair were rolling around on the floor like tumbleweeds. A towel that was most likely used to extricate the cat from Mrs. Stanley lay crumpled up in the corner.

"I know this has been a very emotional and stressful experience for all three of you," I began. "I'd like to offer my help if you're willing. Maybe together, we can figure out a direction to go from here."

"Put the cat to sleep," Mrs. Stanley stated firmly.

Mr. Stanley reached down and pulled the blue carrier closer to his side of the room, almost as if his wife's very words could carry out a death sentence.

"Come on, Judith, you're talking about *killing* my cat. Can't we at least discuss it together?" Mr. Stanley looked over at his wife and then back down at the carrier.

Ebony was the only pet in the Stanley home. He had wandered up to their back door over a year ago. Despite Mrs. Stanley's reservations, they adopted him, and he became an indoor/outdoor cat who spent a lot of time outside with Mr. Stanley when he worked in the yard.

"He's a flea hotel with shark's teeth," announced Mrs. Stanley. "Whenever I get out of bed or step out of the shower, he bites my ankles. And he sheds so much. I'm forever chasing him with the brush, but he hides. He hates it, but I can't have all that cat hair everywhere in my house."

As we talked some more about life in the Stanley household, a picture was developing. This wasn't an aggressive cat. Rather, several different problems that had more to do with the Stanleys than with Ebony were occurring. Ebony was just reacting to what was being dealt to him.

The behavior Ebony was displaying at home by biting at Mrs. Stanley's ankles and feet was most likely play aggression. When directed at appropriate toys that behavior is acceptable, but when directed at a human or other companion animal it isn't a good thing.

For Ebony, the sudden appearance of feet in motion was too irresistible to pass up. Upon delving further into the story, I discovered that the biting occurred when Ebony was kept in the house for long periods of time. Ebony was a highly energetic cat without adequate outlets. He loved to hunt, often stalking and pouncing on anything that moved, be it a leaf, twig, or unfortunate moth. The only playtime offered indoors, though, was on rare occasions with Mr. Stanley, who was adding to the problem by using his fingers to entice and tease the cat. By using fingers as toys, he was teaching Ebony that it was permissible to bite skin.

Behavior Plan

- ❏ **Hands off.** Fingers are never to be used as toys. Mr. Stanley needs to change the way he plays with Ebony and use interactive toys from now on. Mrs. Stanley also needs to engage in interactive play to help reduce Ebony's biting and provide proper energy outlets.

- ❏ **Where's the party?** Set up things in the house to make indoor life more interesting. Use puzzle feeders, solo activity toys, boxes, and so on, to enrich the environment. Ebony needs more fun in his life.

- ❏ **Achieve new heights.** Set up a cat tree near a window to give the cat something to climb on. Not only does this provide much-needed activity, it also makes a great vantage point for checking out the birds, which is highly stimulating for most cats.

- ❏ **TLC.** To help a cat learn to enjoy grooming, start slowly. Sessions should consist of one or two light strokes down the back, followed by whatever type of petting he enjoys. Gradually increase the number of strokes, but always finish before the cat becomes uncomfortable. In Ebony's case, Mr. Stanley is to do the grooming at first, but eventually Mrs. Stanley will be able to resume the brushing duties, provided she changes her technique to be gentle and positive.

- ❏ **Pay day.** To help the cat learn to enjoy grooming, use clicker training during grooming sessions. After stroking one time with the brush, click the clicker and pay the cat off with a small treat or a bite of wet food. Gradually increase

> Cats naturally enjoy hunting for food, so puzzle feeders are a great way to create a fun activity. You can make a homemade puzzle feeder with a simple cardboard box. Tape the box closed and then cut several paw-sized holes in random places. Toss some dry food or treats in there that your cat can reach for. You can also buy commercial puzzle feeders in pet retail stores.

> If your cat hates to be groomed, reevaluate the type of tools you're using. Short-haired cats may prefer the soft, massaging feel of a rubber-bristle brush. Long-haired cats need a relatively soft-bristle brush in addition to a comb.

the number of strokes and then pay off again. Pretrain the cat using the clicker training method described in chapter 1.

- ❑ **Happy trails.** To reduce a cat's anxiety about veterinary visits, get him comfortable with the carrier beforehand. Leave the carrier out in the cat's area so it loses its negative associations, and line the inside of the carrier with a towel to create a cozy bed. Try feeding the cat near the carrier, and periodically toss some treats in. Also, take the cat for very brief car rides around the block and back so that a trip in the carrier doesn't always end at the veterinary clinic. Because of Ebony's history, when the Stanleys do have to take him to the vet, they should schedule the appointment for a time when the clinic isn't so busy to reduce Ebony's wait in that scary place.

If your cat gets very fractious at the veterinary clinic, ask the receptionist if you and your cat can wait in your car rather than in the waiting room. If you have a cell phone, the receptionist can call you when it's time. It's also helpful to avoid typical busy times, such as Saturdays. Here's another tip: Spray the inside corners of the cat carrier with Feliway Comfort Zone spray twenty minutes before putting the cat inside. The pheromones in the spray can help your cat feel more relaxed during transport.

Follow-Up

Ebony now accepts and even welcomes grooming. Mrs. Stanley said that Ebony purrs when she brushes him. They've come a long way. Whew!

The play aggression biting has ceased since Mr. Stanley quit using his fingers to tease and instead uses interactive toys. Getting enough stimulation every day also helped put an end to this behavior.

And, finally, by engaging in play sessions with Ebony, Mrs. Stanley's heart has warmed up to the black cat. One night when Mr. Stanley was in the recliner, Ebony curled up next to Mrs. Stanley on the sofa. But let's keep that our secret—we don't want to ruin Mrs. Stanley's tough image.

CHAPTER THREE

CATS AS INTERIOR DECORATORS— furniture scratching

People try everything to get their cats to stop scratching the furniture. And therein lies the problem. They're trying to get their cats to *stop* doing something the cats know they *should be* doing. To a cat, scratching is as natural as hunting a mouse, grooming himself after a meal, purring, or meowing. It's as natural as breathing.

Scratching serves many vital functions for a cat: For one thing, it conditions the claws by removing the outer dead nail sheath. It serves territorial purposes, too, leaving both a visual mark and an olfactory (scent) mark (from scent glands located in the cat's paw pads). So there's more to scratching than meets the eye.

Another less obvious (but certainly no less important) benefit of being able to scratch is that it serves as an emotional outlet. You may notice that the time your cat chooses to scratch the furniture is when you walk in the door after being gone all day or while he's anxiously watching you prepare his dinner.

I assure you, there are ways to train your cat to use a scratching post. Not all posts are alike, though. Some are great and some aren't even good enough for firewood. For a scratching post to be a success, it must meet four requirements: (1) sturdiness; (2) proper height; (3) appealing material; (4) good location.

Many scratching posts fail on all four points, especially points 1 and 3. Before you buy a scratching post, put your hand on top and try to wiggle the post. If it's too wobbly or the base isn't substantial enough, it could topple over—not appealing for kitty. Materials are important, too. People often choose a carpet-covered post because it looks nice and matches their décor. Unfortunately, that carpet is too soft to do the job a cat needs. Stop thinking *soft* and start thinking *rough*. Sisal, a strong white fiber used to make cords and twine, has an ideal texture for scratching posts. Sure, it may not look as pretty as a plush carpet, but it will look better than having your furniture shredded.

VERTICALS AND HORIZONTALS

One evening at a fund-raiser, a veterinarian came over and introduced himself to me. We'd spoken on the phone many times, but Dr. Biondi and I had never met.

"If you have a minute, could I talk with you?" he asked.

He wanted to find out how things were going for a client of his whom he had called me about several months earlier. The client, a woman in her late thirties named Andrea, had a nine-year-old male cat, Rudy, who had been tearing up her furniture for most of his life. Apparently, her attempts at training had consistently failed, so eventually she just gave up and surrendered her furniture to the cat.

Dr. Biondi had first called me about Andrea when she came to him to discuss having Rudy declawed. She had recently gotten married, and Michael, her new husband, didn't want the furniture he brought into the marriage to get destroyed (a reasonable request). Since his sofa and living room chairs were in far better condition than hers, they'd gotten rid of her damaged furniture.

Andrea told Dr. Biondi that within hours, Rudy had scratched the sofa. In a panic, Andrea tried to cover it by tossing a few pillows on the sofa with the explanation that they added a decorative touch. But Rudy was just getting warmed up. He was born to scratch, and now he had all this unmarked furniture on which to work his decorative magic. Michael's sofa and chairs soon resembled their predecessors.

Dr. Biondi tried to discourage Andrea from declawing Rudy. He asked if she had a scratching post for him, and she replied that she had them all over the house but Rudy totally ignored them.

Andrea and Michael wanted to buy new furniture, but they knew it was impractical as long as Rudy had claws. Time was running out for Rudy because Michael wasn't as attached to him as Andrea was and wasn't as tolerant of his destructive tendencies. The cat had to be declawed or he'd be restricted to the outdoors. Andrea was beside herself because Rudy had been an inside cat from the time she first brought him home.

When Dr. Biondi first called me regarding Andrea and Rudy, I asked him to find out what kind of scratching posts she had purchased. I recommended that she try a sisal-covered post. I also recommended that she place the post right next to the sofa and cover the sofa and chairs with sheets, making sure all of the ends were tucked in securely.

I also instructed Dr. Biondi to give Andrea my usual speech emphasizing that she shouldn't punish Rudy for scratching the sofa, but instead reward him when he used the post. I felt that a change to a better post would make a difference and that Andrea would see positive results soon.

A week later, I received another call from Dr. Biondi. Andrea had purchased the type of scratching post I'd recommended and had covered the furniture as I'd instructed. But not only had Rudy continued to ignore the post, he'd started to scratch on the carpet—something he hadn't done before. Declaw surgery was scheduled for the following week. As I grilled Dr. Biondi for more details so we could figure out what was going on, I learned that Rudy wasn't scratching along the sides of the sofa and chairs, only on top of the back and arms.

"It sounds like we have a *horizontal* scratcher. That's what the problem has been all this time. I'd better talk with Andrea," I said.

I arranged a house call, and once I got there I realized why Michael was so upset. Freddie Krueger couldn't have done a better job at slicing and shredding the furniture. In fact, no one in the house was happy. After being disciplined repeatedly for scratching, Rudy was now avoiding Andrea altogether. He'd become afraid of the one person in his life who should represent total trust and love. And, of course, this was hard on Andrea, too.

The damage to the sofa and chairs was just as I'd expected. The back and sides of the furniture were untouched and all the damage was confined to the tops and the cushions. Rudy was indeed a horizontal scratcher. That's why all of the scratching posts weren't of interest to him. They were all *vertical.*

"Most cats scratch on vertical surfaces," I explained. "For instance, out in the wild a cat would probably scratch on a tree. That's why we simulate trees indoors with scratching posts. But some cats do prefer horizontal scratching. We just need to turn Rudy's verticals into horizontals."

Behavior Plan

- ❑ **Think on top of the box.** Try corrugated cardboard scratching pads. They come in various shapes and sizes, and many are treated with catnip for added enticement. Place the pads next to the furniture currently being scratched and over any scratched spots on the carpet.

- ❑ **Sticky situation.** Place strips of Sticky Paws (available at pet retail stores) along the top of the sofa or other favored scratching areas. Warn people that the tape is there, so no one gets an unexpected surprise should they sit down and lean back only to have their hair get stuck to the sofa. No one ever said cat training was pretty!

- ❑ **Kiss and make up.** If discipline about scratching has been an ongoing dynamic, use an interactive toy with the cat to ease any hesitation or fear. Playing on and around the scratching pads will also guarantee that a claw or two finds its way into the cardboard. Once a cat experiences the feeling of the cardboard, especially during the excitement of playtime, he'll want more. As he realizes he's no longer being punished for scratching, he'll eventually become more relaxed and the relationship will begin to repair itself.

> Interactive playtime with a fishing pole–type toy is a great way to build trust with a cat because it puts just enough distance between you. It ensures that kitty doesn't feel threatened and is comfortable to enjoy the fun experience, laying the foundation for a positive association.

- ❑ **A new perspective.** Try placing a vertical scratching post on its side so the cat can scratch horizontally. Sometimes, you can eventually stand the post back up vertically and the cat will continue to scratch on it. In Rudy's case, I'm not sure he'd be open to something new after nine years of horizontal scratching, but it's worth a try.

> Periodically rub a little catnip on the scratching post as an added treat for your cat. It's a terrific way to create interest in a forgotten post.

Follow-Up

Rudy loves his horizontal scratch pads and hasn't put a claw to the furniture or carpet since. He didn't like the vertical post, so Andrea and Michael replaced it with a terrific sisal-covered scratching pad. Rudy and his claws are *very* happy—and so are Andrea and Michael.

Using your imagination is sometimes the best way to solve a behavior problem. Not all cats read the manual on how to be the typical cat, so you may have to look for a not-so-typical solution. There's always a solution out there, you just have to find it—sometimes it's vertical and sometimes it's horizontal.

MAKING YOUR MARK

Theresa Alvin thought she had her cat figured out. Conway, a sweet seven-year-old, had always been the perfect cat. He was playful, affectionate, and friendly to all of Theresa's guests, and he never misbehaved.

Originally from Chicago, where they lived in a high-rise apartment, Theresa and Conway moved to Nashville, where she was finally able to buy a home of her own. Conway seemed exceptionally happy with his new location. The house provided lots of room to play and hide. And having windows that looked out on a yard opened up a whole new world for Conway, who'd seen nothing but sky and clouds previously. He spent hours watching the birds in the trees. Theresa was thrilled to see her cat enjoying life so much. She even put up a birdbath in the backyard to add to Conway's entertainment. He loved it.

Unfortunately, in addition to birds, the birdbath also drew other, less welcome visitors to Theresa's backyard, namely, the neighborhood cats. It was when she heard a banging at the window that Theresa first saw how popular her birdbath was with the local felines. She came running from the bedroom to find Conway standing up on his hind feet, slapping at the window with one of his front paws. Theresa got to the window just in time to see a big orange cat running from the yard with a bird in his mouth. Two other cats were sitting near the birdbath, waiting for their opportunity to catch lunch. "I'm sorry, Conway," she said. "I think I'll have to get rid of the birdbath." The next day, Theresa sadly dismantled the birdbath and put it away in her garage.

With the birdbath gone, Theresa thought her problem with the neighborhood cats was over. Well, for her it was, but for Conway the memory was a bit more difficult to shake. Theresa first started to worry when she noticed Conway running over to the window, turning his back to it, and getting into a spraying stance. So far all he did was a lot of tail twitching, but Theresa knew it wasn't a good sign.

For the next week, Conway continued to back up to the window and twitch his tail, and even though he hadn't yet sprayed, he was making Theresa nervous. "If you're going to do it, will you just get it over with and stop torturing me?" she asked her startled cat one night after watching him twitch his tail for what seemed like the three-hundredth time. Conway's only response was a throaty meow. The next morning she called the veterinarian. "I can't stand it any longer," she said. She was given my number.

Conway's mock spraying seemed to occur whenever he was unsure where to direct his energy. The move to the new house certainly opened up a whole new world for him, but it also created new anxieties. Thus far he'd been content with just going through the spraying motions without actually spraying, but Theresa wasn't sure how long her luck would hold out.

One thing I noticed as I toured Theresa's house was that Conway didn't have a scratching post, despite some furniture looking like it had been scratched a bit. That gave me an idea.

Behavior Plan

- ❑ **Room with a view.** Even though the birdbath and outdoor cats are gone, the negative association is still there. Blocking the view may help. Temporarily block access to a troublesome window by covering it with cardboard or another opaque material. Closing curtains or shades may be sufficient if the cat doesn't show any interest in climbing up under them.

- ❑ **Turn that frown upside down.** Play with the cat in the problematic area on a daily basis using an interactive toy to help facilitate positive associations. Daily interactive play therapy sessions will also help direct the cat's energy and restlessness toward something positive. In addition, provide him with a cat tree or elevated perch that overlooks a neutral window so he can still enjoy looking outside.

- ❑ **I've got better things to do.** Create activities and use puzzle feeders to entertain the cat when he's alone. When I visited Conway, I noticed that he enjoys peeking out from under things, so he's a good candidate for cat tunnels and hiding places.

- ❑ **The sweet smell of success.** Place a Feliway Comfort Zone diffuser in the room. Its feline facial pheromones may alleviate some of the cat's anxiety in that area.

Soft-sided cat tunnels are available at pet retail stores, or you can create your own by cutting openings in the bottoms of paper bags and then taping the bags together.

- ❑ **Scratching the surface.** Make sure the kitty has a few scratching posts, and be sure to put one in the room with the troublesome window. Since scratching can also be a displacement behavior, providing an outlet for anxiety, it might provide the cat with a more positive emotional release. Perhaps Conway would be satisfied to mark his territory by scratching.

Follow-Up

The addition of a scratching post and cat tree provided Conway with the outlet he needed. His desire to mock-spray was satisfied by being able to happily scratch on his post. Whenever his energy started getting the best of him, he zoomed up and down his cat tree, which served as a signal for Theresa that it was time for a play therapy session. She was able to remove the cardboard from the windows a few weeks after my visit, and Conway now vigorously scratches his post whenever he sees a strange cat outside.

WHAT'S MINE IS MINE

What do you do if you have the most stubborn cat on the planet? What else is left after you've tried every kind of scratching post? What do you do when your cat still thumbs her little nose at her post? Horizontal, vertical, rope, carpet, bare wood—nothing works. Your cat still insists on clawing things she shouldn't.

I experienced such a cat when I met Hannah, the two-year-old black-and-white female owned by Donna and Rick Catalano. Hannah was the most recent addition to a household that already included three other cats. Rick had rescued Hannah two months earlier when he found her nearly frozen to death underneath his car in the driveway.

Two months and several vet visits later, a healthier Hannah had become an official member of the Catalano family. The other three cats appeared to handle the change with a minimum of complaints. A confident trio, they let Hannah know right away that they were in charge. Hannah accepted her position in the family, and within a short time, hisses, growls, and paw slaps were few and far between.

Donna and Rick called me to their house to figure out if there was any way they could train Hannah to use a scratching post. The three other cats used scratching posts, but Hannah chose to scratch on doors, walls, and even the brick fireplace hearth. As much as they didn't want to declaw her, if Hannah didn't change her ways Rick and Donna were going to do it.

During the consultation, I asked Rick and Donna if they'd ever seen Hannah use a post, even just once. "In the very beginning she did," answered Rick, "but she'd get chased away by one of the other cats. They weren't used to her being in the house yet."

In my tour of the house I saw three well-worn scratching posts and three cardboard scratching pads.

Looking at the places Hannah chose for scratching, I noticed they all seemed to be in neutral areas—places that didn't seem to be of territorial concern to the other cats. For instance, Hannah scratched the door to the upstairs guest room, the closet door near the front door, and the fireplace hearth. She also scratched on the wallpaper in the dining room, and even on the legs of one of the chairs. Rick said that it was the one chair that none of the other cats used. The other three chairs had cushions that Donna had made, but she hadn't gotten around to completing the one for the fourth chair.

As I toured the house, I began to see that the three original cats had long ago established ownership of the six scratching surfaces, and they remained quite territorial after Hannah arrived. As I questioned Rick and Donna further, they started to recall seeing particular cats routinely going to specific posts. By the time Hannah came onto the scene, no one was willing to share. After being chased away repeatedly by the other cats, Hannah got the message and decided to find alternative places to scratch.

Behavior Plan

- ❑ **A post to call my own.** Purchase a new sisal scratching post for new feline additions to the household.

- ❑ **Sock puppets.** In order to help the cat identify with her new post and let the other cats know who it belongs to, mark it with the new cat's own scent. To do this, put a pair of socks on your hands and rub the cat gently around the face. Then distribute those facial scents on the new scratching post by rubbing it all over with the socks.

- ❑ **Repeat performance.** During the first week, freshen the scent if necessary, performing the sock puppet rubdown again, first on the new cat, then on the post.

- ❑ **Party at the post.** Have play sessions with the cat around her post using an interactive toy. Initially, place the post on its side and dangle the toy around and over it. Sequester the other cats in another room so the new cat can play uninterrupted.

- ❑ **Stick to the point.** To discourage the cat from going back to scratching on walls or other off-limits surfaces, cover the scratched areas by taping on long sheets of paper. Then, place strips of double-sided tape on the front of the paper so the surface will be sticky and unappealing to kitty's paws. It may be easier to cover certain scratched areas with slick paper, such as poster paper, or a plastic carpet runner. The paper can be removed after the cat's scratching habits are firmly redirected toward the post.

A plastic carpet runner over a scratched area serves as a deterrent. Use a runner with pointy nubs, and place it with the points facing up.

Follow-Up

Having a post that didn't already carry the scents of the other cats made it easier for Hannah to feel comfortable using it. The sock rubdown accelerated it becoming her own personal territory. She now scratches on her post and shows no interest in the walls, hearth, or furniture. Within two weeks, the paper and plastic runners had gradually been removed from the walls and furniture.

> Any time you use a deterrent such as a carpet runner to stop scratching in a certain area, provide the cat with other options. Scratching is a natural behavior, so be sure to give your cat other acceptable options for doing it.

CHAPTER FOUR

behaviors that befuddle, frustrate, and melt your heart

Some cat owners have the good fortune not to experience any behavior problem more unusual than keeping the cat from jumping on the counter. Then there are those who are given a little extra challenge in life. Although some behavior challenges can truly test your patience, try to keep your sense of humor and remember the love you have for your cat. No matter what all the neighbors tell you, your feline companion is *not* a psycho kitty.

FASCINATING FAUCETS

Some cats develop a fascination with particular items. It could be a spot on the wall that your cat never gives up on, forever believing it to be an elusive bug. Or it could be certain movements on TV. One of my clients has a cat who guards the VCR, intently watching the blinking digital time display. While such irresistible objects usually occupy only a small portion of a cat's busy schedule, there are those single-minded felines who relentlessly pursue the object of their desire, almost to the point of being unaware of life around them.

Spencer is a perfect example of such a cat. This two-year-old tabby had a fascination with water. It's not uncommon for cats to enjoy watching a dripping faucet, occasionally pawing at the water. Then there are those cats who refuse to drink water from any source other than a running faucet. For too many owners, what began as a cute little game of laughing at your kitty as he played with the dripping water becomes the water-on-demand syndrome, meaning that when the cat wants water, he sits by the faucet and waits for his ever-faithful owner to turn it on for him. Some cats are very lucky to have such well-trained owners!

For Spencer, merely playing with the drips from a faucet or a melting ice cube on the kitchen floor wasn't enough. What started out as an amusing curiosity soon crossed the line into a full-time quest. Spencer constantly had to be around running water.

When Spencer was just a kitten, his owners, Bill and Nancy Brock, thought it was so cute the way he'd climb up their legs and sit on the kitchen counter to watch the dishes being washed. To amuse Spencer between dishwashing times, Nancy would turn on the faucet so drops of water would slowly fall. This soon became the routine not only in the kitchen, but also in each bathroom.

The Brocks even nicknamed Spencer "Drippy." In time, he lost all desire for any activity other than eating, and even that was done hastily so he could return to the faucet. Eventually, he began sleeping by the sink.

Several veterinarian visits determined that there was no medical cause for Spencer's behavior. The Brocks, though not pleased with his obsession, were willing to tolerate it—that is, until his behavior began taking a rather frightening turn.

It began with unlatched doors. Spencer was content with dripping faucets and the regularly scheduled melting ice cubes in his water bowl, but if he heard a faucet running or toilet flush from behind a closed door, he'd meow, claw at the door, and if it wasn't securely latched, he'd barge right in on some unsuspecting soul. Spencer had no regard for anyone's privacy when it came to his water-watching needs.

During the next few months, as long as everyone securely closed the bathroom door, Spencer appeared resigned to his daily ritual of watching Nancy do the dishes. But peace in the Brock household was only temporary. Spencer was making plans, and his obsession was about to reach new heights.

One morning after Bill had gone to work, Nancy headed to the bathroom for her morning shower. She undressed, turned on the shower, and stepped in. A few minutes later, she felt a slight draft. Figuring she hadn't latched the door and that Spencer had pushed it open, she readjusted the water temperature to take the chill out of the air. Then, out of the corner of her eye, she noticed the shower curtain move slightly. "Must be the draft," she told herself and proceeded to shampoo her hair.

The shower curtain moved again. Nancy stuck her head out to see how far open Spencer had pushed the door. She reached out and pushed the door closed, noticing Spencer wasn't in sight, then ducked back into the shower.

Nancy heard what sounded like a sneeze. She peeked out from the shower and called Spencer, but didn't see him. Then she heard a second sneeze. Once again she stuck her head out from the shower and scanned the bathroom. "Spence?"

"Meow," came the reply.

Sitting in the shower directly behind Nancy was a soaking-wet Spencer.

"Spencer!" Nancy screamed, throwing open the curtain, then she jumped out and grabbed a towel, her heart beating wildly. She reached back in the shower to turn off the water, figuring Spencer must've bolted, but there he sat. Nancy looked with bewilderment at her cat, who was staring up at the last few drops of water clinging to the showerhead.

Determined to be more diligent about latching the doors, the Brocks continued to tolerate Spencer's fixations—that is, until the *second* shower incident. This time the victim was Bill's mother, who was visiting for a few days.

Not being a cat lover, Bill's mother, Elena, wasn't thrilled to find Spencer suddenly right next to her whenever she came close to a faucet, whether she was getting a glass of water or brushing her teeth. She'd been warned about the cat's behavior, and although it perturbed her, she was willing to tolerate it during her visit—until the third day of her visit. It was early on Sunday morning, and Elena couldn't sleep any longer. She decided to take her shower while waiting for Bill and Nancy to wake up. She turned on the shower to warm the tub before getting inside.

While waiting for the water to heat up, Elena went into the guest bedroom to get her clothes. When she returned to the bathroom, she shut the door behind her carefully, pulling on it twice to make sure it was securely closed. Bill had even put a sign on the door warning guests to be sure to latch the door. Elena mumbled to herself about how foolish her son had become over a cat.

Elena took off her robe, hung it on the hook behind the door, and then removed her eyeglasses. The warm water felt good as she stepped into the shower. Closing her eyes, she let the water cover her head, when suddenly she felt a little tickle on her right ankle. She looked down but saw nothing except the swirling water.

She had begun shampooing her hair when she felt another tickle, this time on the other foot. She looked down again. For a second, she thought she saw a flash of something dark by her foot, but without her glasses her vision wasn't very good.

When it happened again, Elena was certain something actually touched her foot. She looked down and squinted her eyes in an attempt to focus. She turned and looked down toward the back of the tub. Nothing. Then the shower curtain on the outside of the liner began to move.

Elena pushed aside the liner to peer outside the tub. That's when she came eye to eye with Spencer, who was hanging halfway up the curtain. Both of them dripping wet, they stared at each other in disbelief for a few seconds before Elena let out a scream. Spencer took that as his cue to drop from the curtain and hide behind the toilet. Elena got out of the tub to physically evict Spencer from the bathroom. Making sure he was truly locked out, she started back to her shower when she heard a worried Nancy and Bill knocking on the door. "That cat has to go," Elena huffed as she pulled the shower curtain back into place. "He's a menace."

I was called for a consultation a few days later. I glanced around the living room, which was crowded with shelves filled with books. The coffee table was covered with papers, file boxes, a briefcase, two laptops, multiple cell phones, and several unidentifiable candy wrappers.

Bill sat down in the chair across from me. "Nancy and I are lawyers. We work long hours both at the office and here," he said as he pushed the papers on the coffee table off to one side, revealing coffee stains, probably from too many long hours of late-night work.

As soon as adequate space was created on the table, Spencer made his appearance by jumping up, sitting directly in front of me, and looking right into my eyes. He blinked slowly, and I noticed tiny droplets of water on his head.

"You've been in the sink again, haven't you?" I asked as I extended my hand for him to sniff.

Another slow blink was his guilty reply.

After getting enough background from the Brocks, I toured the house (including all of the faucets) and spent time with Spencer. His love of water was the most extreme I'd ever seen in a cat. But after spending a good amount of time with him, I got the feeling that water was Spencer's only source of entertainment in that house.

"We don't have any time. That's why we got a cat; they're supposed to be less trouble than a dog," Bill admitted.

I took Bill and Nancy on a tour of their own house so they could see it through Spencer's eyes. They finally realized just how uninteresting their home was for a cat. There weren't any elevated spots for perching, and Spencer didn't have access to any window. Almost every surface was covered with stacks of books and papers, and Spencer was immediately reprimanded if he attempted to land anywhere but the preapproved counter by the sink. No one ever had time to play with him. I couldn't locate a single cat toy anywhere in the home. The poor kitty didn't have anything to play with but water.

Behavior Plan

- ❑ **Time off for good behavior.** Conduct play therapy sessions with the kitty a couple of times each day. Stalking and chasing an interactive toy will be much more interesting for him than watching water drip from a faucet. He needs appropriate stimulation to divert him from the faucet and toward the right type of games. The interactive toy will also satisfy his tactile desire to touch and capture his prey.

- ❑ **The buddy system.** A second cat can provide much-needed companionship for a single kitty, especially if his owners are often gone or busy. The Brocks should consider adopting another cat to ease Spencer's loneliness during his many hours alone.

- ❑ **Real estate investment.** Add a cat tree or some window perches. Since there obviously isn't an unused surface in the Brocks' house for Spencer to sit on, he needs some furniture of his own.

- ❑ **Activity time.** Set up fun solo activities to allow the cat to discover that the dry side of life can be fun. Use puzzle feeders or hide dry food in small dishes around the house for him to find. And, for goodness sake, make sure he has toys. I think Spencer would enjoy the light plastic toys made to resemble milk jug rings. Their movement is irresistible.

- ❑ **Water show.** To safely indulge a cat's love of water, set up a pet water foundation, which uses a small aquarium pump to circulate the water. There are several brands on the market, and they're widely available at pet retail stores.

> If you buy a pet water fountain, be sure to take it apart frequently and clean all nooks and crannies so the water stays clean. Change the water regularly as well. Stale water isn't tasty.

- ❑ **Bait and switch.** Use play therapy to distract the cat from his fixation on running water. Since Nancy tends to pile the day's dishes in the sink until after dinner, when she rinses them off and loads the dishwasher, in the Brocks' case this means Bill will take Spencer into the bedroom or office at that time for a play therapy session. This will help break the pattern of having him sit by the sink during dishwashing time.

- **Favorite movies.** No, I'm not suggesting that a cat might enjoy watching *Gone with the Wind*, but there are several cat-entertainment videos on the market. These videos showcase prey in natural settings, and many cats find them very appealing.

Cat videos are available at many pet retail stores, as well as online, and many cats love them. They usually feature birds, insects, mice, and fish. One of my cats' favorites is called *Video Catnip*.

Follow-Up

Spencer is no longer interested in the kitchen faucet or any running water for that matter, other than his own personal water fountain, which sits on the floor near his food bowl. The Brocks bought him a cat DVD, and he loves to watch it, especially when it comes to the sections that showcase fish (no surprise there!). They also set aside daily play-time with Spencer, and that has strengthened the bond between them and allowed them to rediscover what a wonderful and fun cat he is.

I helped the Brocks find a companion cat with a personality I felt would be compatible with Spencer's. Bill and Nancy came over to meet little Ruthie, and she won their hearts. The now-enlarged Brock house-hold is happy again—well, almost. The bad news is that Bill's mother still won't come for overnight visits anymore and prefers to stay in a hotel instead. (And actually, Nancy confessed to me that not having her mother-in-law stay overnight wasn't really such bad news after all.)

DON'T PET PICKLES

"My cat won't let me into my house!" a woman screeched into the phone. "I opened the front door and he lunged at me. I called my veterinarian, and he said to call you. Can you come right over?"

"I'm in the middle of a session right now," I replied. "I'll phone you as soon as I'm through."

The woman was not pleased. "You don't understand," she said, enunciating excessively for effect. "I cannot get into my house! I'm sitting in my neighbor's kitchen. I have groceries in the car."

I looked back at my clients, who were patiently sitting in their living room waiting for me to return. "I'll be there shortly," I sighed.

As I pulled into Marion's driveway, a woman came running out of the house next door with another woman following right behind her. From the serious look on the face of the first woman, I assumed she was Marion Estee and that the second woman, with a rather amused look on her face, was her neighbor.

"Thank goodness! Oh, thank goodness," Marion called out as she came around the front of my car and yanked open my door before I'd even turned off the engine. "Nothing like this has ever happened before. I just can't believe he's doing this!"

"Hold on for a minute," I said, putting my arms up to prevent her from pulling me along. "Before we go in there, I need to get some background on what happened."

"I came home from doing my grocery shopping. When I put the key in the lock and opened the door, Pickles was standing right there growling at me with a glazed look in his eyes. I tried to open the door a little more so I could get in and calm him, but he lunged at me. He made this awful screaming sound. I backed up and slammed the door. I could still hear him carrying on from behind the door. I waited and then tried to

go inside again, but as soon as I opened the door he lunged at me again." Marion looked over at her neighbor as if for comfort and then continued with her story. "I decided to go around to the back door, but as I opened it, Pickles was right there. He jumped at me. I shut the door and went to the garage," Marion said, her voice starting to quiver again. "The only other way in is through the door that connects the house to the garage. I tried to be very quiet, thinking Pickles would still be standing by the back door. But I had barely opened the door when he threw himself at me. I managed to get him off my sleeve," she said, pointing to her left arm.

"Has Pickles ever done anything like this before?" I asked.

She shook her head. "I haven't had him very long. I officially adopted him about three weeks ago. He used to hang out by my back door, waiting for food. I'd leave a dish out there for him, and then he finally got brave enough to come in. I figured he had been somebody's cat. Maybe he had gotten lost or somebody dumped him for whatever reason. I put an ad in the paper, but nobody called. He seemed like an okay cat." Marion paused and looked back at the house with a frown. "That is, up until today."

"Has he been to the veterinarian?" I asked.

"I haven't gotten around to it yet."

"Are there any other pets in the house?"

Marion shook her head. "It's just me and Pickles."

I instructed Marion to stay outside while I attempted to go inside and see Pickles. First, I went to my car and took out a blanket in case I needed to protect myself from any possible lunging attempts. I also brought along a cat carrier.

I walked up to the front porch and peered in the window. Pickles was sitting in the middle of the living room with his head hanging low. There appeared to be feces spread across the carpet. Then he just flopped down. Whatever the crisis was, it appeared to be over. Pickles looked exhausted.

As I opened the front door, Pickles turned and looked at me. I could see that he had also urinated on the carpet, and from where I stood, it appeared he'd gotten a significant amount on himself, as well.

I took a few steps closer. The cat stood up, and with several twitches of his skin, walked off toward the kitchen, but it didn't take long for him to reappear around the corner.

He hesitantly walked over to me and rubbed his head along the back of my hand. I was concerned that the skin twitching might indicate some sort of physical problem, so I was very careful as I petted him behind his ears and under his chin. No skin twitching so far.

At the sound of a small dog barking outside, Pickles' ears perked up and he bounded over toward the front window. With a graceful leap, he jumped onto the wide windowsill to get a better view. Everything seemed normal, but then his skin started twitching again. I moved nearer to the window, being careful not to distract him.

As I got closer, I saw that the twitching was getting severe as Pickles paced back and forth along the windowsill. I also noticed something else. The bottoms of the light, lacy curtains repeatedly swept across his back as he paced. His lashing tail kept catching them, causing the fabric to slide back and forth along his spine. The more this happened, the more his skin twitched. Pickles began to emit loud growls and moans. Within seconds, he dropped from the windowsill with his ears laid back and started tearing around the room.

As quietly as I could, I reached behind me and grabbed two sofa cushions to shield myself with as Pickles raced toward me, totally out of control. I held the pillows in front of my face and heard the sound of teeth meeting fabric. At least it wasn't teeth meeting flesh . . . my flesh.

It was all over in a few minutes. I slowly lowered the pillows and saw Pickles sitting on the carpet a few feet away from me. His chest was heaving and he looked quite dazed. Moments later, he was walking around again and growling. Ten minutes later he was acting as if nothing happened.

I walked out of the house and back to an anxious Marion to report what had happened.

"Why is he doing this?" she asked.

"There could be a number of reasons. It may be a condition called hyperesthesia, but this can only be diagnosed by a veterinarian after a careful evaluation.

"Hyper *what*?" Marion asked, nervously chewing on a fingernail.

"Basically, it's an excessive sensitivity to touch. The problem can present itself as unprovoked aggression. Other conditions, such as spinal problems, pain, skin problems, or epilepsy, need to be ruled out first. The veterinarian may refer you to a specialist so an MRI can be done." I saw that Marion was getting increasingly impatient; perhaps she was adding up the cost of all of this in her head. "First, let's get Pickles to a veterinarian to discuss the options."

We went into the house, and I was able to get Pickles into the carrier while Marion phoned a nearby veterinarian's office to let them know we were on our way.

When we arrived, I went into the examination room with Marion and Pickles to be sure all of his symptoms were accurately communicated to the doctor.

The outcome of all the tests was that Pickles didn't have epilepsy, spinal problems, a skin condition, or any injury that would provoke such sudden aggression, so he was referred to a specialist for an MRI.

As I'd suspected, the diagnosis ended up being feline hyperesthesia syndrome, which occurs due to a neurotransmitter malfunction. It's similar to what humans experience as panic attacks. Hyperesthesia most commonly appears in cats under five years of age, but it can occur in older cats. Cats under stress are at greater risk.

Armed with the correct diagnosis, the veterinarian, along with the help of a veterinary behaviorist, began Pickles on a treatment plan that involved the use of antianxiety medication.

Behavior Plan

- ❑ **De-stress.** Some environmental changes are needed. Create elevated areas and hiding places for a stressed-out cat.

- ❑ **Music to my ears.** Keep a radio on during the day to act as a buffer for outdoor noise or other sudden sounds that could trigger the cat's anxiety. Tune the radio to a station that plays classical or other soothing music and keep the volume relatively low. A multiple CD player can be loaded up to play hours of soft classical music.

- ❑ **Windows on the world.** Get rid of anything that causes unpleasant sensations that could trigger an aggressive episode. In Pickles's case, this means removing the curtains. To block off the window so Pickles can't see the neighbor's dog, Marion can install shutters. Since she's always wanted them anyway, this is a good time to get that done. Marion can use the shutters to keep Pickles off the windowsill while still keeping the top half open so sunlight can enter the room.

- ❑ **One-on-one.** Use play therapy to help relieve stress. Play sessions also help strengthen the owner-cat bond.

With cats who are easily agitated, keep play sessions from becoming frenetic. Play the way a cat would naturally hunt, allowing for both mental and physical engagement. Don't drive the cat to exhaustion with nonstop movements.

- ❑ **Hands-on.** Be aware of the cat's sensitivity when you pet him. Stroke him gently, not briskly. With Pickles, Marion will only stroke around his head, not down his back.

- ❑ **Get a job.** Set up activity toys and adventures for the cat when he's at home alone. He needs fun and satisfying things to do to occupy his time during the day.

- ❑ **It pays to learn.** Start doing some clicker training work with him to help mark the relaxed behavior. That way he'll learn to focus on the positives that earn him a reward.

- ❑ **Air-conditioning.** Use a Feliway Comfort Zone diffuser to help the cat relate to his environment in a calm way.
- ❑ **I spy.** Become more aware of the cat's body language to detect any tension or the possible onset of an aggressive episode.
- ❑ **The glare of the spotlight.** If the cat seems agitated, turn off the lights and darken the room. The less stimulation the better, so as to avoid triggering an episode.

Clicker training should be fun, so choose times when your cat is rested. He should be hungry but not starving. Train in short sessions, and don't show frustration if your cat isn't responding.

Follow-Up

Pickles is monitored by the veterinarian and veterinary behaviorist on a regular basis. His antianxiety medication has been adjusted a few times, and now he's on a lower dose. The behavior modification plan has had a positive effect on Pickles. These days he's relaxed around company and is more receptive to physical affection. And best of all, he and Marion have developed a special, loving relationship.

SOCKS APPEAL

Many cat owners have seen it, heard it, and been driven nuts by it—wool sucking. It's the strange behavior some cats display that consists of sucking and kneading on anything from the corner of a blanket to the hair on an owner's head. This behavior is named wool sucking because many cats focus this activity strictly on wool or wool-like fabrics, such as blankets, sweaters, and socks. The owners of cats who occasionally suck on a shoelace may think it's cute, but those whose cats relentlessly suck on blankets and expensive sweaters come to me at their wit's end.

What is wool sucking, and why are some cats fixated on this bizarre oral behavior? One theory is premature weaning. Wool sucking mimics nursing, including the milk tread, the kneading motion kittens do with their paws to stimulate release of milk from the queen. The idea that wool sucking is caused by premature or abrupt weaning seems valid to me, because many of the cats I see for wool sucking were rescued or adopted at an early age, under eight weeks old—too early to be separated from their mother and littermates.

A cat named Wishbone was referred to me by a local veterinarian because of her overpowering need to suck on her owner's clothes. She'd had a complete exam and workup, and the vet determined that she was in perfect health.

When I knocked on Vanessa Teague's apartment door, I was met by a young woman holding a pair of socks out in front of her. The red socks looked quite wet, indicating a very recent crime.

"My roommate forgot our rule about not leaving clothes out. She left these on top of the dryer this morning." She transferred both socks to one hand and shook them in the direction of the mixed-breed cat that had sauntered up to the door. "You're a bad cat, *bad cat!*" she scolded, then turned her attention back toward me. "You see what we're up against?" She held out her hand, the one without the socks. "I'm Vanessa and that's Libby, my roommate, over there." She gestured toward the young woman sitting on the sofa. I couldn't help but notice the outfit: red shirt, red and black checked pants and . . . bare feet. I assumed the socks she had planned to wear this morning were now crumpled in Vanessa's grip.

Wishbone was a one-and-a-half-year-old cat Vanessa had picked up in the parking lot at her office when she was just a kitten. The veterinarian had estimated her age to be about five weeks at the time.

"She used to just suck on shoelaces, so we didn't think anything of it," Vanessa said.

"But then she graduated to blankets and any clothes we left out. At first I thought she was peeing on them, but they didn't have any smell."

"Follow me," instructed Vanessa as she stood up and motioned to me. I was led into a bedroom where there was a chair blocking the door to the closet. "We had to put this in front of the door because if the closet isn't latched just right, Wishbone can open it."

As Vanessa moved the chair aside, Wishbone was right there, true to form, ready to make the most of the opportunity. Libby reached down and scooped Wishbone up so Vanessa could open the closet door. As I looked inside, I noticed the rod was exceptionally high, obviously a measure they'd resorted to in order to keep Wishbone from reaching the clothes.

"I'm about at the end of my rope," confessed Vanessa.

Behavior Plan

- ❑ **Don't tempt fate.** Keep all laundry put away. Dirty clothes should be kept in a hamper with a lid, and all clean clothes should be kept in closed drawers or closed closets. Don't leave anything available. Once the cat has been trained, these measures won't be necessary, but in the interim it will make the transition as easy as possible for the kitty.

- ❑ **Patience is a virtue.** Cease all punishment. Since this behavior is truly out of the cat's control and may be triggered by anxiety, don't add fuel to the fire. Punishment is *never* an appropriate form of training.

As cute as it may appear at first, don't encourage your cat to suck on fabric, fingers, shoelaces, her own tail, her paws, or other objects. Although it may seem innocent at the outset, it has the potential to become a compulsive behavior, especially if the cat's environment is stressful or unstimulating.

- ❑ **A mouth on a mission.** Occupy the cat's time with more interesting and constructive behavior. Set up puzzle feeders and other activity toys for her to enjoy. Make sure her environment offers plenty of stimulation. This will help reduce her anxiety and boost her confidence.

- ❑ **Girl talk.** Spend more time playing and interacting with the cat. She needs at least two play sessions a day to keep building her confidence. The more confident she feels through successful mock hunts and the more positive experiences she has in her environment, the less likely she is to turn to a sock or blanket for comfort.

As cats mature, they often outgrow wool-sucking behavior, provided they don't live in a stress-provoking environment.

- ❑ **Timing is everything.** Whenever it looks as though the cat is about to engage in sucking behavior, divert her attention toward a toy. Timing is important: the diversion must occur *beforehand* so it doesn't reinforce the unwanted behavior.

Follow-Up

After one week, Vanessa called with an update. Wishbone's wool sucking had decreased by almost 90 percent. Early on, there was one incident involving the sleeve of a sweatshirt that was left dangling out of the hamper, but after that things got back on track. One year later, Wishbone has continued to be a reformed wool sucker and Libby has happily gone back to her habit of tossing her clothes on the floor. Vanessa told me she wishes she could come up with a behavior modification plan for Libby that was as effective as Wishbone's.

EEK'S BEST FRIEND

Willy, a sixteen-year-old dog, loved sleeping late in the morning. Then, after enjoying a leisurely breakfast of his favorite senior food, he'd stroll outside to catch a few rays. His owners, Wanda and Arnie Tansmore and their young daughter, Angela, all doted on him.

Another member of the family who cherished Willy was Eek, an orange-and-white tabby about twelve years old who shared the Tansmore home with him. Eek had been adopted after Arnie and Willy found her in a ditch by the side of the road one evening during one of their late-night walks. About two years old at the time, she'd apparently been hit by a car and had managed to crawl to the ditch by the side of the road, where she collapsed. After an eleven-day stay in the veterinary hospital, the cat was well enough to be discharged and begin her long road to recovery from two broken legs.

As soon as Angela, also two years old at the time, caught sight of the double-splinted cat, she shrieked "*Eek!*" From that point on, she continued to shout "Eek!" whenever she saw her, and thus the orange cat officially came to be known as Eek.

From the moment Eek was brought home, Willy stayed by her side. Eek slept in the warmth of Willy's soft fur and was groomed by his big sloppy tongue. They became best friends, and for the next ten years, they were almost of one mind. They patrolled the yard together, ate together, and slept just as they had from day one, with Eek nestled in Willy's fur.

Fast-forward ten years to the winter Nashville experienced several ice storms. This particular afternoon started out with a steady rain. Willy had been at the veterinarian for an exam to keep tabs on a developing heart condition. Arnie had dropped him off that morning and was to pick him up at 4:30. Deprived of her buddy, Eek had been very

restless and distracted. She paced and paced, stopping only to look out the window or check for signs of Willy's return.

When Arnie drove to the clinic, road conditions were deteriorating, but he was a careful driver who knew how to handle ice. Upon his arrival, the vet gave Arnie a new prescription for the dog. Arnie scheduled a follow-up appointment, and the two left for home. Unfortunately, the roads were covered with black ice by that time.

Arnie drove as carefully as possible, but halfway home another driver lost control and crashed into the passenger side of the car. Arnie's injuries weren't too serious, just cuts and bruises, but he was badly shaken up. When he regained his composure, he looked over at Willy, who lay motionless. The right side of the car was completely crumpled, and Willy hadn't survived.

The loss of Willy was unbearable for everyone. While Arnie, Wanda, and Angela tried to comfort each other, Eek quietly continued searching for Willy, keeping watch at the window, and pacing the house at night. He hardly took time to eat.

One afternoon two weeks later, there was a sudden commotion in the driveway. Arnie was walking toward the house with a tiny, squirming bundle that emitted a high-pitched yapping sound. Angela came running out of the house with Wanda right behind her. As soon as Angela saw that the mysterious bundle was a golden retriever puppy, she squealed with delight.

Eek watched the sudden burst of activity from the front window. When she saw the puppy scamper up the steps and into the house, she took off to the safety of the bedroom. Arnie and Wanda tried to help Eek become friends with Bob, the new puppy, but their attempts were met with hisses, swats, and long episodes of hiding. For Eek, life now

consisted of being chased, pushed, knocked down, and relentlessly badgered by the exuberant puppy.

Several weeks later I was called for a consultation. As I interviewed Wanda and Arnie, Bob bounced around the room, his tail wagging in excitement. The pup had no idea why I was there, but he certainly was thrilled to have a visitor in the house.

When I went into the room where Eek was hiding, I was immediately struck by her appearance. Even taking her age into consideration, the cat I was looking at bore little resemblance to the one in the photographs around the house. This cat was thin and had dull, dry fur. Her eyes appeared vacant. She sat like a statue on top of a tall dresser in the bedroom—her usual spot according to Wanda. No wonder, I thought to myself, it's the one spot where the dog can't get to her.

While the Tansmores had thought they were doing the best thing for their family by getting a puppy to ease their grief, they created a worse situation for poor little Eek. For this stressed cat, who was still grieving for her lost companion, the sudden appearance of a puppy was unwelcome and ill-timed. Eek lost every remaining semblance of security as the puppy just bulldozed right over her. Her life became a day-to-day search for a safe place to hide.

I tried to explain this to the Tansmores gently: "Eek needed recovery time, and she needed your attention to let her know that everything in her life hadn't changed. And don't forget that she's an older cat. An energetic puppy can be too much."

"Eek needed us and we let her down," Arnie said, shaking his head.

"Eek still needs you now, and you can be there for her," I said as I watched the puppy begin to chew on the corner of my briefcase. "Let's start right now—with Bob."

Behavior Plan

- ❑ **The doctor is in.** Arrange for an appointment with the veterinarian right away to rule out any underlying conditions.

- ❑ **Teacher's pet.** Consult a qualified, certified dog trainer to help control that irrepressible bundle of misdirected puppy energy. Most dogs require proper obedience training; without it, they'll become the kind of pets no one likes.

- ❑ **Take two.** Reintroduce the two pets in a way that respects the cat's personal space. She has a right to feel safe in her own home. For example, Eek never got the chance to decide whether she could ever like Bob or not. From the moment he entered the house, she had to go on full security alert. Beyond the fact that Eek is still grieving for Willy, the puppy is simply too intrusive. The reintroduction process involves clicker training and positive association. Eek and Bob should start by being in the same room, but at opposite ends, and Bob should be on a leash. Armed with treats and dog toys, the Tansmores need to get Bob not to focus on Eek, but rather to relax and focus on them. The more quickly Bob learns that ignoring the cat will earn him a reward, the faster Eek will accept him.

- ❑ **Remember me.** When a new pet joins the family, preexisting pets need exclusive time with their owners. The Tansmores must make time for Eek each day. That time could include play, petting, grooming, or anything that Eek enjoys.

- ❑ **Personal property.** Make sure the cat has plenty of areas of refuge that are off-limits to the new dog.

Follow-Up

Bob went through obedience training and is a perfectly behaved dog—well, almost. He responds to verbal commands, and "Stay" has been most useful in helping Eek learn to accept Bob in her life. While the bond wasn't the same as the one that she had with Willy, she did begin sleeping with him. Instead of curling up against his chest the way she did with Willy, she chooses to snooze on top of Bob. Thrilled that she views him as a comfortable bed, Bob doesn't even mind when her tail tickles his ears.

Eek's initial physical exam was unremarkable except for the veterinarian recommending that she be given vitamins because she had lost weight. Between the behavior modification program and the healing power of time, Eek continued to improve emotionally.

Three years after Willy's death, Eek was diagnosed with a cancerous tumor. Despite the best medical care, her prognosis was very grave. Wanda and Arnie agonized over what to do. After watching their precious cat steadily become weaker, they finally made the painful decision to end her suffering. Wanda called the veterinarian and made an appointment for the next morning.

Eek never made it to the veterinary clinic. She quietly died in Wanda's arms that evening, surrounded by the family that loved her so. The next day, Arnie dug a grave, and Eek was buried alongside her beloved Willy so he could once again watch over her.

When dealing with the loss of a pet, remember that your other pets need to go through their own grieving process. Spending extra time petting and playing with them can help make it a less traumatic and lonely transition period for all of you. Engaging in play activities can help a grieving cat feel as if not everything in her life has bottomed out. Try to create a normal everyday routine, paying close attention to providing casual, fun, and comforting activities for your cat.

A LESSON IN LOVE

Before ending this chapter on perplexing behaviors, I thought I'd include a story about an owner's out-of-the-ordinary behavior. And since this book has focused on undesirable and frustrating feline behaviors, I wanted to end with the story that truly reflects the unconditional love that can happen between cats and humans, especially when it's least expected. This love enables us to find solutions to our cats' seemingly mystifying behaviors and enables our cats to endure our often clumsy attempts at communication.

Mr. Vinsley was one of the most memorable clients I've ever known. Originally from England, he was an older man who had been a widower for many years and lived in a beautiful mansion in Kentucky.

"My problem is very unusual," he said at the beginning of our phone call, and he refused to go into any greater detail.

"I prefer to have an idea of what behavior a cat is displaying in case I feel a visit to the veterinarian is needed," I responded.

"I promise you, a veterinarian is not required for this situation," he replied.

The Vinsley residence was located on a beautiful and secluded road. The long driveway led up to a magnificent house.

I was greeted at the door by the housekeeper, who eyed my armful of cat toys and raised an eyebrow. I was ushered into the living room to meet Mr. Vinsley, who stood when I entered the room. A very distinguished-looking man, he appeared to be in his seventies. He wore a three-piece suit with a stiffly starched shirt.

I began to question Mr. Vinsley about his cat. "What behavior has your cat been displaying?" I asked, preparing to take notes.

"Oh, he's a fine cat," he stated. "There's nothing wrong with his behavior."

"All right, then. How can I help you?" I asked, somewhat confused.

"I need you to find a good home for my cat."

"Mr. Vinsley, I don't handle animal adoptions. I deal with cat behavior problems. I can give you the names of some wonderful people I know who—"

"No," he interrupted. "I specifically want *you* to find him a home."

"Why me?"

"I've read your books, seen you on TV, and heard about the work you do. You really understand cats. My cat, Dancer, is all I have, and I want the very best for him. I'll pay you for all the time you spend searching."

"Why do you need to find him another home?"

Mr. Vinsley looked at me for a long time before opening his mouth to answer. "I have cancer," he said, almost in a whisper. His doctor had told him he had less than nine months to live. He was not afraid to die, he assured me. After all, he had lived a good seventy-seven years. He had every comfort, had never wanted for anything, and was willing to face the end of his life with dignity. All of his business was in order. He had no family and wanted the money from his estate to go to cancer research, children's charities, and several animal-welfare organizations.

"There's just one important thing left to do," Mr. Vinsley said sadly. "I need to take care of Dancer. I found him four years ago, and we've been best friends ever since. I need you to find him a home while I'm still alive. I want to know for sure that he'll be getting the love and care he deserves. I'll provide for his medical and food expenses. He has been by my side through these very tough last years. When I was too sick to get out of bed, Dancer stayed right with me. He's a wonderful friend, and I want to make sure he lives a good life without me."

I didn't know what to say. Mr. Vinsley stood up, breaking my awkward silence.

"I'll introduce you to Dancer." With that, he left the room.

It was then that I realized I'd been holding my breath as he'd been talking. I hadn't been expecting anything like this.

A few minutes later Mr. Vinsley came back, holding a cat in his arms. Dancer was a tough-looking male cat who had obviously seen more than his share of fights before becoming a resident at the Vinsley home. He was a huge cat—not fat, but large. Both ears were torn at the tips and his nose bore several old scars.

Despite his rough exterior, Dancer's personality was sweet and gentle. Wrapped in his owner's arms, his loud purr sounded like an old car engine.

Mr. Vinsley had found Dancer sitting on his car one cold winter morning. Having no fondness for cats whatsoever, he promptly chased Dancer off the car, and that was that—or so Mr. Vinsley thought. But every morning for the next week, he found the gray cat sitting on the roof of his Mercedes.

One morning as Mr. Vinsley watched the news on TV from his bed, he heard that the temperature would continue to drop during the day, and that it would be frigid by evening. Even though he didn't like cats, he hated the thought that the poor creature might freeze outside. He quickly dressed and went out, fully expecting to find the big gray cat lounging on his car as usual. He opened the front door, felt the blast of cold air, and looked out. No cat.

When the housekeeper arrived home from her morning shopping, she found Mr. Vinsley in the kitchen in his robe, spooning a can of tuna into a dish. She didn't ask him what he was doing. He hadn't been eating well lately, so if he wanted to eat tuna at seven in the morning, why bother him?

Mr. Vinsley hurried outside and placed the dish of tuna on the roof of his car, then went back to his warm house to wait.

By the end of the day, the tuna, now quite frozen, was removed from the car. The housekeeper watched but knew better than to say anything.

"Have it your way, you stupid cat," Mr. Vinsley said as he went back inside the house and dumped the can in the garbage. Just before going to bed that night, he stuck his head out the front door one more time to check for the annoying cat. He wasn't out there, so Mr. Vinsley locked the door and went to bed.

At about 2:00 a.m., Mr. Vinsley woke up. He swears it was a terrible thirst that drove him out of bed and down the stairs to the kitchen. Along the way, he stopped for a quick peek out the front door—still no cat sitting on the car. But just as Mr. Vinsley was about to close the door, he caught sight of something limping toward him. Hobbling up the driveway was the gray cat. His fur was matted and dirty, and his right front paw dangled helplessly in the air. Mr. Vinsley stepped out onto the porch, but as soon as he did the gray cat stopped.

"I'm not going to hurt you," he said to the cat. "Come here and I'll help you."

The cat just looked at him, not moving. Mr. Vinsley didn't know if he should go in to get more food. What if the cat ran off? But he knew he had to do something soon—the cold air was going right through his thin robe.

Leaving the front door open, he slowly stepped backward into the house and padded into the kitchen, where he dumped some leftover chicken onto a large plate. He was afraid the cat would be gone, but when he got back to the front porch, there the cat was, standing in the driveway with his paw in the air.

Mr. Vinsley placed the food on the porch and leaned against the doorway. The old man and the cat just looked at each other.

"I generally don't care for your kind, you know," Mr. Vinsley said to the hesitant feline, "but please let me help you. Come on, it's too cold for me to be out here."

A few minutes passed. Mr. Vinsley was shivering. The cat was watching him intently; he seemed to be making a decision. Warily, the gray cat limped up to the porch, sniffed at the plate of food, then weakly hobbled past it and through the open doorway.

After some hesitation, the cat allowed Mr. Vinsley to examine his injured paw. It would need medical attention first thing in the morning. In the meantime, the scruffy thing would spend the night in the kitchen. As Mr. Vinsley bent down to scoop him up, the cat hobbled off on his three good legs in the direction of the stairs. Before he could be stopped, he clumsily ascended toward the bedrooms.

Following him up the stairs, Mr. Vinsley found that his furry houseguest had decided the master bed was the perfect place to sleep. He was already curled up at the foot of the huge bed.

"You could have at least chosen one of the guest rooms," Mr. Vinsley commented. But he was too tired to argue, so he crawled under the covers, stretched his feet out next to the cat, and turned out the light. "Don't get too used to this. You're leaving in the morning."

The following morning on the way to his own doctor's appointment, Mr. Vinsley dropped the cat off at the nearest veterinary hospital.

That very visit to the doctor was when Mr. Vinsley learned he had cancer. Depressed and frightened, he drove home, almost forgetting to stop at the vet's. In fact, when he realized he was about to pass the animal hospital, he seriously considered just leaving the cat there for the vet to deal with. But he stopped anyway.

The gray cat had a broken leg. When the veterinary technician brought him out, he was sporting a large splint. Mr. Vinsley paid the bill and left with the cat.

Three weeks into this new relationship, Mr. Vinsley's health took a serious turn for the worse and he was confined to his bed. The cat, by now named Dancer because he could move so gracefully despite his heavy splint, left Mr. Vinsley's side only to use the litter box and eat a generous amount of food.

Their friendship grew deeper and deeper. When Mr. Vinsley was well enough, the pair would stroll around the grounds or sit in the sun. Dancer loved to sleep in Mr. Vinsley's lap as he listened to classical music or read a book.

As I listened to Mr. Vinsley talk about Dancer, I promised myself I'd do everything I could to fulfill his wish.

After a lengthy search, I found a potential home for Dancer: Ruth Leeson, a very sweet and gentle woman who had lost her husband years earlier. I thought it was a wonderful chance for Dancer to give this lonely person the same gift of love he'd given to Mr. Vinsley.

When Ruth met Mr. Vinsley and Dancer, all three of them hit it off. They spent quite a bit of time together, and Mr. Vinsley took great pleasure in telling Ruth all about Dancer's likes and dislikes.

Eight months after I first met Mr. Vinsley, he was taken to the hospital. His housekeeper phoned to tell me that Mr. Vinsley wanted me to come get Dancer and take him to his new home. I canceled my appointments for the day and then called Ruth to tell her to expect Dancer.

I drove to the Vinsley residence. The housekeeper let me in and I collected Dancer's things. As if he knew what was about to happen, Dancer was waiting for me in Mr. Vinsley's room. He sat quietly on the bed.

Later that day, I visited Mr. Vinsley in the hospital to tell him that Dancer was in his new home and that Ruth was doing everything she could to make him feel at home. He smiled. We talked a little while longer and then he drifted off to sleep. I quietly got up and stood by the bed for a few moments. "I'll keep watch over Dancer for you," I whispered, and left him to rest.

Two days later Mr. Vinsley died.

I've since visited Dancer in his new home several times, and he's very happy. He follows Ruth the same way he did Mr. Vinsley. And I've noticed that Ruth looks much more content than when I first met her. She proudly told me that Dancer sleeps on his own pillow next to her in bed.

Dancer, the once scruffy, tough stray cat, taught Mr. Vinsley how to love again. And now the furry gray teacher with torn ears and a purr like an old car engine is helping Ruth learn that same lesson.

FINAL THOUGHTS

For most of us, cats are graceful creatures, loyal companions, and the most intuitive friends in our lives. Yet, for others, cats are frustrating mysteries, tigers in tabby clothing, and totally unpredictable animals unable to be pleased. I hope this book has helped ease some frustration for those of you who feel that every day is a battle against that four-legged ball of fluff who often has you scratching your head. Do you ever wonder though what our cats think of us? I wonder if they find us to be confusing, moody, chatty, scary, and inconsistent.

In our relationships with our cats, they're the ones who actually do the most compromising, adapting to our rules even when they don't make any sense to the cat, and even if we continually change the rules from day to day.

In the wild, a cat has a few simple requirements: water, a mate (if lucky), a tree or two for marking and climbing, a little soil for those personal functions, and a modest supply of prey to catch. Then we come along and suddenly it's "Don't climb there . . . Don't scratch on that . . .

Don't pee there . . . Don't chase that . . . Don't shed . . . Don't meow." In essence, "Don't be a cat!"

If you start to look at things through your cat's eyes, you'll find solutions to behavior problems. As with any relationship, it comes down to communication.

If you feel you're unable to handle a behavior problem, there is help out there for you. Start by consulting your veterinarian, who may be able to help. In addition, your veterinarian may then refer you to a certified animal behavior consultant, a certified applied animal behaviorist, or a veterinary behaviorist.

Don't worry; you don't have a psycho kitty. You have a kitty who is trying to tell you something. Listen to her.

INDEX

PHOTO CREDITS

Pedigree Pets photographed by ImageSource/ Getty Images, pages vi, x, 7, 8–9, 18, 35, 36–37, and 71.

Fuzz-Buzz and Kona photographed by April Orcutt, pages 4 and 50.

Oni, Bivvy, Sam, and their couch photographed by Betsy Stromberg, pages 5, 31, 60–61, 73, 75, 106, and 109.

Pepper photographed by Christy Westmoreland, pages 10 and 14.

Lunesta photographed by Jessica Nelson, page 27.

Bebe and Mary Margaret photographed by Pam Johnson-Bennett, pages 39, 45, and 97.

Annabelle and Savannah photographed by Julie Bennett, pages 48 and 53.

"Black Panther" photographed by Stefano Tiraboschi, ©istockphoto.com, page 56.

"Sisters at Rest" photographed by tiburonstudios, ©istockphoto.com, page 59.

"Cat Marks" photographed by AllSearchingEye, ©istockphoto.com, page 64.

Trixie photographed by Joanna Shober, page 67.

Bluebirds photographed by David Westmoreland, page 69.

Ramona photographed by Rachel Moore, pages 76–77.

"Chat assoifé" photographed by Manon Allard, ©istockphoto.com, page 78.

"Clean Kitty!" photographed by Spauln, ©istockphoto.com, page 83.

Black cat photographed by red2000, ©ImageVortex, page 88.

Dog and cat friends photographed by bhochmuth, ©ImageVortex, page 99.

"Golden retriever" photographed by Simon Mitchell, ©istockphoto.com, page 100.

"Hide and seek" photographed by Peeter Viisimaa, ©istockphoto.com, page 112.

ALSO BY PAM JOHNSON-BENNETT

TWISTED WHISKERS

Solving Your Cat's Behavior Problems

7 x 9 inches • 178 pages

ISBN-13: 978-0-89594-710-9

0-89594-710-2

30,000 COPIES SOLD!

Available from your local bookstore, or order direct from the publisher:

Crossing Press
an imprint of Ten Speed Press
PO Box 7123, Berkeley, CA 94707
800-841-BOOK • fax 510-559-1629
www.tenspeed.com • order@tenspeed.com